The Lost Book of Barkynge

The Lost Book
of Barkynge

Ruth Wiggins

Shearsman Books

First published in the United Kingdom in 2023 by
Shearsman Books Ltd
PO Box 4239
Swindon
SN3 9FN

Shearsman Books Ltd Registered Office
30–31 St. James Place, Mangotsfield, Bristol BS16 9JB
(this address not for correspondence)

ISBN 978-1-84861-863-3

Contents

Cry out, therefore, and write thus.
                              —Hildegard von Bingen

Be silent no more. Cry out with a thousand tongues – I see the world is rotten because of silence.
                              —Catherine of Siena

Foreword

In his *Historia ecclesiastica,* Bede refers to a 'libellus' (or *little book*) compiled at Barking Abbey in the early 8th century, but which is now lost. When I first encountered the ruins of the abbey on the banks of the River Roding, I was overwhelmed by a sense of those lost voices. And slowly what had begun as a handful of poems about a favourite river became *The Lost Book of Barkynge* as first one nun and then the next demanded to be heard. The book traces the history of the abbey from its foundation in 666 to its dissolution in 1539. It includes extensive notes that I recommend to the reader as integral to the text. Barking was a royal abbey and was a centre of learning for women at a time when few other opportunities existed beyond marriage. The poems are an attempt to recover the voices of the nuns, abbesses and local women of the period. They offer a conjectural history but one grounded in thorough research, and though not an exhaustive list, all the abbesses are mentioned in the historical record. Each section begins with a 'hic' (*here* or *this,* in Latin) to set the scene of the period. These lyric captions offer a different slant on the usual bullet points of British history. Barking itself is in what we would now call East London but was historically an ancient parish on the Roding, north of the Thames. There is a marginal note (c.1000) saying *'þis is seo boc to Beorcingon'* / 'this is the book for Barking Abbey'. In the words of Lisa M.C. Weston in her essay 'The Saintly Female Body and the Landscape of Foundation in Anglo-Saxon Barking' this 'book' marked 'the transformation of secular, dynastic *folcland* into monastic *bocland* and it is the inviolable space of that book-land, and the potential it offered the centuries of women that lived there, that this collection endeavours to explore.

Ruth Wiggins

And so begins nine hundred winters

— 7th century —

A rose of shimmering – Æthelburh

And so begins in England, a hundred winters of raising holy villas Æthelburh's brother, soon to hold the bishopric, founds two   one at Chertsey for himself, one at Barking for his sister   Days of Cædmon and Hild, mother of snakestones at Streoneshalh   Æthelthryth at Ely, her sister Wendreda the healer   The daughters of Eafe   Mildrith, Mildgyth, Mildburh   Miraculous escapes across a river   protectors of springs and of barley, birds

At Lundenwic the Thamesis cannot move for ice
        cold on her bed and
                        drifting towards release
            Æthelburh remembers

Miracles

The translation of unexpected bones
                at the raising of Berecingchirche
        Earconwald baptising a goste-lyfe
                        releasing him to dust
            with just
        the holy water of his pity

This abbey raised
        for her and for her daughters
                        and for the daughters after
            From Francia dear Hildelith to guide them

But since they first broke ground
        bright lights in the sky   sickness   inundation
                        a great palsy among the geese
            men labouring in a storm of clay
                    at Berecingum and Certesi
        The sun hiding its face
            signs and portents   but how to read them

reading   in itself an answer   a mistlethrush
           tru-truing in the holly

She hums the old liturgy   remembers the sky fires
       that brought the yellow plague
how they seemed to chase upon the heels of glaziers
                     here from Gaul
      to teach the art of windows
Apertures into crystal   crysoprase and sard
        How bloody rain fell
           milk and butter turned to blood

Earconwald's letters   urging
    gather your daughters seclude them
       Instead
    they opened their doors to the flood
       In all charity
    how could they not

Pestilence

Even the boy Æsica on whom the sisters doted
      and none more so than sweet Eadgyth his teacher
       little Æsica   taken
With his last earthly breath he called to Eadgyth
    Eadgyth!   three times he called
          once for each of his too few years
   and wondrous! at prayer   that-very-moment   Eadgyth
         did also call out
     and then did follow him
    that he would not have to step
          into the light alone

Green the child in the earth no more to
   hurry into lessons
       Green in the earth and sweet

o puzzle
soon to join him

We intercede for the dead

Now Earconwald   here you come again
    come to die at Berecingum
                    Dear brother   conveyed
                            in a horse-drawn crib
    Old Hæsl   steady mare   she too
                outlives you

The brothers at Certesi and from the Bishopric
            all noisy for your body
    cloak   staff   your everything   all carried off
                        No quiet relic left to honour
                a sister's loss
        How we sunk our hopes
                        into that sudden rising
            of the river
    remarkable flood   apparent   interceding
            but then a miracle
        with which we virgins
                    could not argue
    a weary trunk   perhaps fallen upriver
        into the flood and
                    staunching
            Easy passage then
            for them to carry you off
        your body to London
            and there   to rest

Bright glade of grass
        a rose of shimmering

This kingdom of the yellow death   its estate pricked out in decades
            O world in turmoil   and people
                    losing faith

A bold comet standing
             and standing   in the autumn dawn
    for months standing
Old Ofwyth gone
    and Thecla
  your complaint in the night at the vigil torch
    moving towards a brighter
               light and gone by dawn

Æthelburh asks the last of her daughters where
      they will have her lay
  their bodies down
             lay down the daughters after
          they say
        they cannot answer
    Then   oracular night! when praying
the still unsettled graves
        tilth freshly leavened by gravel
          spade
    Of a sudden   a great sheet of light
sky like wool   combed
       by a great weft beater
          billow lifting from the loom
            then dipping
    south and west of the chapel
        where it does hang   in plain view
          of each astonished handmaiden

And Æthelburh has her answer

Shucked and cast away – Tortgyth

And Tortgyth who knew Æthelburh as a child at court   came south
with her Barking not so different from the wetlands of Lindsey   both
bounded by marsh and river, birch trees   A cloister of birdsong and
midges   unceasing choir   their bellies full of garnets   But as when an
oyster has been shucked and cast away   the shell goes brittle   and one
half finds itself worked free of the other

     We were as sisters   embroidery
                  scripture
         plaiting each other's hair   always together
Æ's good father
        knew from the start
              offered her   crown or psalter
      but like her brother
   she had no use for gold

He had us learn together
        and when the time came we left as one
we took the dyke and then
        the long stræt south
   until
as pilgrims working our soft way
        through fen
we found the tracks of brushwood
        pocked with flint

The look on her face   bittersweet and shy
       that first day when she raised   as Abbess
         the sacramental shears
  my hair coming away in her hands   no need of cutting
    body so eager to be humble
       just   the ritual of her fingers

Not yet the pain this struggle with no release
    nocte os meum perforatur
                doloribus
          by night my bones gnawed with it
     Even the cunning woman
          at Dæccanhaam   her leather bib
              hung about with beads   little buckets
      even she cannot help   it is the Lord's work
Excruciation is an impious noun   but   Mother of God
      it has been nine years now
              the tight intricacy of my body   consumed
       I am the garment
    eaten away by moths
 et quasi vestimentum quod comeditur
             a tinea

Awake through the night   perpetual office
    stumbling yesterday   terrible numbness
Craving   usefulness

      I swing my legs out of this cot
           thin   no more than kindling
  step   down   onto the whispering
         rush-bed floor
I tell the hours with this   body   am a liturgy
   joints   a buc of   shells
          eight steps   from cot to door
     each   a station

Outside   the night damp grass   soft about my knees
   my woolly robe
           my face skyward
I am brittle in a dark wool cloak
             a white puck where my twin
     might have held

But what is this   there!   in the sky
            longhaired and in a white robe
    drawn up   up
            on golden cords of virtue
                        brighter than the moon
            a miracle of light that rolls in the air
                sleeves folding in a cascade
                    of white
                            towards the earth

It is Æthelburh   my dearest friend in all the world
            her habit as though hung about with
                    weights   and yet   aloft
    her hair long   no longer shorn
            restored

What does it mean
            it must mean soon
                    soon   she will be
                            gone

    And what
            not take me with you

Seigneur en jupe – Hildelith

It is the age of the daughters of Cynewise   abbesses Cyneburh and
Cyneswitha and their kinswoman Tibba in her falcon feathered cloak
All raise houses of their own   Their brother Æthelred, and Sæbbi, king
of Essex endow Barking with land   The abbey is growing   Sacred relics
come from Francia   brought by Hildelith from the abbey at Chelles

Là! un chat sauvage
    she breaks from the birch trees
        goes skittering across the ice of the marsh
    frozen all the way
    from here to Dæccanhaam
the pasture a winter monstrance
    une merveille   that holds
    in reliquary   the life of the grass
    all fodder
a relic   in the winter dawn

    There the fertile marsh   pasture   *banque de gravier*
    navigable creek & pool
    moulin à grain
La rivière en été   grosse de sole

Not for me the scrollwork of the sky
    instead the useful mystery   *des maisons royales*
    this easy age of saints
des pèlerines pushing through fen
    tracks of brushwood pocked
    with flint
I will have to pay the marsh men

I am she through whom the grain flows
    a skirted lord   *seigneur en jupe*
it is cold   children splashing there   beyond the mill
    not two weeks past

and now iced over
tout mes sources fraîches en Toi

I must shore up this place
against incursion   dismissal
pour les sœurs   who will come after
that they be free *d'adorer et de lire*
et de protéger
les âmes de leurs ancêtres

I came to teach the goodhearted daughter of a lord
très faim du mot
together we have built a haven
en psaume   et en brique
the application of the Rule
la discipline

Æthelburh   we miss your light touch
last week   again!   *deux!*
novices
working gold into their hems
Alors! these girls   still hankering
d'ornements du monde
How did you manage them
they don't love the difference in me
they like to mention
their dowries
And hound's teeth! I've had it with Berngith
that trick *avec les œufs*   and her blue teeth
Lord but she is
funny

We have built upon your *bonnes œuvres*
and grown a sanctuary around you
you   and dear silent Tortgyth
I was with her
when   *miraculeuse!*   her tongue unlatched

It was timely   your return for her
          her bones
                scarcely stitched together
          but we are now but twenty   Scholastica gone
                and oh   *la peste jaune*
                     How to keep this space
                we cannot survive alone on   *chansons*
                          pour les morts
                intercessions   dowries
                la Messe

          I'll not be a fragile rib
               I will write   reach out

Letters – Hildelith

Britain is an island of many tongues   one common, by virtue of scripture
Little curls are scraped from holy books   given in water to assuage an
ague   News of a translation   the relics of Æthelthryth, queen of the
Fens   monks sent through marshes to find a new coffin, boat low in the
water with miracles   The congregation of Ely sing   the blind rest their
heads upon her coffin, to see again   The shore is ringed with mussels
pearls of purple, white and green   an abundance of whelk, from which
a red that neither fades nor bleeds

Aldhelm salve

Please
speak of our subtle industry
our litheness with scripture
perspicacious
exquisite battle
we dive into the river
of its meaning

Know us as your bees
chaste and busy
with the sweetness
of the Word
happy in our hive

Speak and gather us
into a modest book
and copy that book
that it be shared in this
house of virgins
and without

From Berecingum to Monkwearmouth – Hildelith to Bede

Yes she was so
very upright in life
our Lady
constant
and always planning

But I must tell you also
of the blind wife
who came
to Æthelburh's burial place
How great a grace
of healing!
She sees again
from simply kneeling
a short while there
in prayer

Lift up your pen
born of the dazzling pelican
and with your eloquence
and wisdom
wind us a pathway in ink

Semper
Hildelith

O how these inks are stilled
by winter
I must warm my pen
Do the larvae not love
the vellum!

I see a storm of birds
thin, angular
beaked in their nest
of interlace
yellow eels, blue horses
There is a hand in the margin
and a beauteous B
alike of Beatus and of
Berecingum

Bede, dear Bede
Rome makes inroads
on our song
inching out the old
melodies
Now, as I write
the choir sing
O Gloriosa
Domina
it is a thing
to hear them

O how to keep
this space
That it be not just a space
that can be razed
It is a puzzle
you boys might
help with

In the name of our
Saviour, commend
us in your letters
where memory might
otherwise
fade
Let us not lose
the light, be wrapped
in dimness
no more the inked
and solemn skin

Let the girls
pinch out
the calf, fill it
with visions
The ink
in this one's hands
seems to lean
towards embellishment

H

These dear bricks

— 8th – 10th century —

i The bloody welkin (for the unnamed)

ii Bright, as with comets falling (Wulfhild – twice abbess)

The bloody welkin – for the unnamed

Fearsome ranks in the heavens   famine on the earth   and then in Dorset   the Norsemen   Tremendous tokens across the welkin   and then, the Norsemen   Fiery dragons gambolling across the firmament, heavy portents   Lindisfarne, Jarrow   London besieged   Northumbria fallen   East Anglia fallen   Edmund martyred   *hic hic hic* in the bracken   And then at Barking the great undoing

in a margin:

Rumours of a great slaughter reach us
Lundenwic besieged
An army
in alliance with winter

The sky again   late winter aurora

This time   three hundred ships
prowling up the Thamesis
their long beaks jostle and leer
along the strand

This time   they
have settled-in
They piss on the old city walls
make raids   sorties
grow bored

They nose into the Roðing

•

glint-boards torn from bóks   pale, go-past pages
reeds and feathers stamped on   wolf-sealed,
bear-trod   the authority of dogs   fires in the sky
and words we cannot

·

Their boats slip easily into our streams
We smell them before word reaches
Quiet through the mist

We are lost   Mother bade us
leave
take the books
take the

·

the big house overcome   its twenty sisters   flame
scrambling up their legs   those mistresses
religious   yellow eels, blue horses   hot dragons
scrambling   their cloaks withstand the fire   for a
moment   their prayers plaiting their way   right
up to the welkin

·

O Christ   O Scholastica
patron of storms   we have need of your sudden rain

The clouds
they do not

break

•

at Mōdraniht in the sleeping   stretched out upon
our beds   husbands snoring, mead-sunk   we,
hægtessan and mægden   helrúnas, burgrúna   go
out through the closed door

we cross great stretches of space with others
winter goddesses, mothers   those who inhabit the
storm, the night, the wild place

spindle and midwif, we ride furious over burial
mounds dyrnecraeft, wiccecræft we call out to
the twenty, the lost   but they wear a caul of mist
and we cannot deliver them

Bright, as with comets falling – Wulfhild

Edgar reigns in peace   For seven years he does not wear his crown
penance for abducting the abbess at Wilton   Two years on and he is dead
Then the martyr-king   and then the whelp-king   but neither have their
father's peace   Bluetooth and Forkbeard devastate the land   this new
kingdom of England unpicked   Bluebells, the like of fire and heady
Manifold disturbances

Angels danced around my
parents. Took their hands,
a holy shower of light. That
I might be conceived and
thereafter a Bride.

Barely weaned and sent to
Wilton, where the young king
did later try to force me. Not
daring to snatch on hallowed
ground he tricked me to Aunt
Whenflæda's banquet.

Running in those foul fine
clothes through the passages
of Hwerwyl, smuggled into a
dark drain and out into a
pathless world.

My return to Wilton, feet in
tatters. Edgar on my heels.
But there, miracles – the sight
of my sleeve in his hand and
he, at last, the model of
remorse. The seam giving
way, as butter.

Still vigilant, I cleaved unto
the altar. Until upon the
reliquary he pledged a
different course, our destinies
entwined thereafter.

In recompense, he offers –
anything. And these dear
bricks are what I ask. This
abbey of terrible ash, I will
raise it from the ground.
I mean for this place, this
time, to last.

Soon the glaziers with their
sheets of ice. As we might
trace a red evangelist or eel,
they conjure out of glass –

Scholastica, this house upon
her palm. Bright crosier and a
dove upon her tongue. Jet
against thunder, celestial
harm.

Oh Edgar, so easily swung.
I am twenty years removed to
Horton, and all for a queen
with a grudge. But lately,
troubled, she dreams of
Æthelburh in rags, squalid,
uncared for… and finally I am
restored.

Last week the milk-eyed boy,
over whose face I made the
cross. My fingers bright, as

with comets falling. The boy's
countenance filled with light
and   now   he   sees.
No need to talk of this,
I hush, *I am but a vessel.* But
the delight of his mother, she
is all chatter. And so, I am
sainted now and old.

Rocks in linen

— 11th century —

With breath and hem – Wulfruna

Candlemas in London, Wulfhild stumbles   As a wall   that has for
some time been leaning   eases into a patch of sun, so she stumbles   her
daughters cradling the blessed light   the bright cups of their hands
Wulfhild carried by a crowd   seven miles back to Barking   to lie beside
her sisters in the brackish ground   Along the way, her body   a stone
and then a feather   joyous portage of mortal remains   The bell ringer,
Wulfruna   known as Judith   is glad to be home   away from the
scolding of the brothers

Not to touch chalice, not to touch wafer
only let its word melt on our tongue.

                    Oh stuff!

Were we not honoured with the intimacies
of shroud and balm?

What do they know of frailty? My chalice
sings like a sky-swung bell,

        I, Wulfruna.

            and they made bells of pure gold, and put the bells
                between the pomegranates upon the hem of the robe

I have no flair with a pen
but I too
have words, *my tongue*

the pen of a ready writer. Not as fine a hand
as the scriptorium girls

who flex their long fingers in the cold, pluck
invisible harps

my thumbs

rough from the jump of the bell rope
the way it leaps faithfully to its task.

a golden bell and a pomegranate, a golden bell
a pomegranate
upon the hem of the robe

No one will miss this scrap of parchment.
Riddled with holes, it can hold

my words

Wulfruna me fecit

•

Here in the stillness, the empty choir
I run my fingers
in the grooves of the aumbry

it creaks. We are of a piece.

Little door I will oil you
unwrap and replace the vessels in you.

A smear on the chalice.

What? Leave it?

I breathe on the gold, mouth half-closed, chin lifted

haaaaaaaaa

work with breath
and hem, till I can see my face in it.

and he made the laver of brass, and the foot of it
of brass
of the looking glasses of the women assembling

•

I am earthenware, keeper of
gold and glass, provider of lights and
keeper of the hours

guardian of the vessels, holy water, blood, bread, book and vestment.

By my hands, the washing of the cloths.
By my hands, the pressing and folding.

For Candlemas, I made thirty candles

lights to lighten

good beeswax, steady.

From darkness bring us, in our good white robes.

Dear Wulfhild, stumbling.
Gold in the bowl of her lovely hands

emptied of their load

o breath of Berkynge.

Revertere, revertere
quene of blysse and beaute

Remedies – The wives

Æthelred has married Normandy   and gift-slain all the Danes in
England   Now comes Forkbeard   a storm of vengeance for his sister
For gold and for Gunhilde   he gathers the north   The abbey goes
into hiding, tall grass sings in the cloister   The women of the village miss
Wulfruna   their sister in the marches, bell ringer   want to tell her of the
Danes who came up river   the wolf that stopped them   These bloody
days of war, England a hog's back bristling with iron

We gather bog moss for bleeding. Swap it for candles,
charms on scraps of sheepskin. Charms that sleep on the
scrap till called into life by the wishing wif who cannot.
Watch the ink now, swaddled. The rise in its chest as she
calls it away from sleep.

Then. Off she goes! Says –

I leap over this dead man's freshly-dug, say *THIS my
remedy for bitter slow, THIS my remedy for will not
grow*

I say this myself

Then. Off she goes! Says–

I leap over you, my cock-hard man, say *up I go, step
over you, with a lively child not a lifeless one, a fat child
not an ill-fated one*

I say this myself

Then. Off she goes! Says –

THIS, by Woden-Christ is done, THIS, by Woden-Christ is done

I say this myself

Then the charm, she tucks it in. Shushes it away to sleep. Now the candlelit lying-in. Sweet caudle to her lips for strength to sip. The mihtig wif, who can.

Boundary – Wulfruna & Merle

And now, tall in the south comes Thorkell   there is mighty assailing
comets, all manner of supernatural   At the siege of Canterbury abbess
Leofrun is taken   The wolf bishop decrees England must fast   Three
days of crumbs, the nation barefoot to mass Then, heart sore at his own
men   Thorkell defects to Æthelred   But London, Oxford, Winchester
all are fallen   And Forkbeard is king of England

These uncertain days, whole months hiding away
we gather the treasures of our church away.

Away, return. Away. We leave the dead to fend…
this dreadful decade.

Today we return to strange account, a month of gifts
from those who'd come to pillage.

Footprints through the house.

and grievous wolves enter among us

A tale told by Merle, running
through the graveyard. Rough Danes

rebuffed at the walls. Oh stout boundary
of clay and lead

an unearthly howl it was, wound up the sky, as
pale red men fell from a skiff, their boots through
the bone yard bent on spoiling, but a wolf! bright
fangs, fierce brow, did hold them

Is not the wolf a defender of the margin.
Does not a wilderness lie beyond.

out of the wilderness like pillars
smoke

the Danes pressed on, but here were won, this spot
where the grey agent of mercy stood her ground,
sacred snarl as she faced them down, hot spittle
singing on the step

O, what a fierce menagerie our founder has
to call upon.

they entered and bowed their heads, returning
later with these gifts, and the lean wolf rejoiced,
her grim evensong, peace to the cherishers of
peace

Pacem cultricibus pacis.

In medio choro – Lifledis

Days of the crown being swapped weekly come to an end   And now
Cnut hangs it on a tree   paddles before the tide at Thorney   He
distributes gifts to atone for the destroying   safe passage for pilgrims
overseas   Churches rise again from blackened floors   England, a crop
of steeples   Alphege's relics are moved to Canterbury   first the longboat
across the Thames, then the long walk through Kent   secured by
awkward, burly guards   They shout *boo* to the monks of St Paul's, who
weep for the lost blossoming

    Wulfhild, it is me, Lifledis.
        Dare I disturb
    your rest? Your body
            long settled.

    Tomorrow we move your relics.

We once fetched water
            together, jugs so
                heavy
    we had to set them down.
                The water-slopped flags
                    of the cloister.
            Do you remember?

You said Greynettle
            was more use than
    the pair of us together
                more deserving
                    of her food by far
            I wish I had
        her shoulders now.

That new mule, bah.

You were sure
          I would be
your successor,
               but who should follow now?
          These new girls
                    know only peace,
where we remember days of terror.

So, tomorrow we shall lift the vessel
          that held you.
                    Pour you out
                              into a safer place.
               By Hildelith
          and our good founder.
The three of you
          together

     in medio choro.

A bundle of myrrh – Wulfruna

Cnut has been to Rome to atone for his sins   he's a Christian king
two wives, one common both called Ælfgifu   elf gift   His southern
queen sees to it that he repairs the monasteries plundered by his kin   he
bestows common land like it's his to give   Thirty years since Wulfhid's
death   the abbess announces the translation of her body   It will be a
new feast, the laity love a good saint   Wulfhild comes to Wulfruna in
a vision, saying   *It will please me if my body be covered with your habit*

Light in my arms, this shroud, spotless
and sewn with roses.

Lifledis has consecrated me to this task.

> *The smell*
> *of thy garments, like the smell of Lebanon*

I lead the procession, steady in my good veil.
I will not stumble.

Such a crowd.

They have come from hereabouts and further
pilgrims through the marsh.

It is a reverend, merie fair.

Waves as of crab apple roll through the churchyard
a spring tide pushing up the Roðing.

Such sweetness.

The smell of thy nose like apples

I lift your incorruptible form,
unaltered these thirty years

where I
am over-wintered.

In death, I am your handmaiden.

> *And my hands dropped with myrrh, my fingers*
> *with sweet smelling*

I lift you.
Tuck you this way and then this.

Settle you, at your own request that you be shielded.

But this scent! It rolls and rolls
till we are giddy with it.

> *A bundle of myrrh is my wellbeloved*

Dear sister, in my liver-spotted arms. Holy bundle,
my hands, they

tremble at this office.

Steady now.

We are to move you from one vessel
to another.

Churchyard to chapel.

The breath with which you spoke,
the breath of apples.

> *A garden inclosed is my sister*

There, you are well wrapped.
But what, they cannot lift you?

Newly gravid as with stones, when in my arms
you were feathers?

We sing the Penitentials, but still
you will not lift.

The crowd surges to lend its strength, but still
not budge an inch.

This mirror of your death.

We pray the burden away, a sinner's hand
heavy upon you.

And then
at last, you lift.

And the bearers take you.

The girl abbess – The choir & Ælfgyva

The island has had enough of peace   So much snow that it crushes the forest   Folk and cattle caught between quakes and wildfire   babes trampled at Dover   Spearhafoc loses the bishopric, makes a run for it bags stuffed with stolen gaudy   His statues of Liudhard and Bertha carried into fields to plead for rain   The king hurls the queen to a nunnery   Ships in the Thames, the king relents   Storms dash the churches, tear up trees   At the abbey, Ælfgyva   kind and full of milk, honey   The bishop comes upon her in passing   ravished by her grace, he makes her abbess

Choir:

Small child of great sweetness, curiosity, wants Cook, wants psalms, wants scrape away at vellum. The Earl says give her everything. Also rigour. Red doves and bricks, one on another. This child's house for birds that they must bring bricks for. Small child of sweetness wants to sleep amid the cooing, bird shit, straw. Wants Cook, wants rigour. Red doves returning, the rain falling soft. Six geese in veils chase the little anchorite out of the storm. You'll catch a chill, that many windowed tower. Wants psalms, wants Cook, wants the story of queen Dido building her walls.

●

Choir:

This girl now a little older, milk, the blush of apples. The fullness of her, lengthened into lean. Still runs about, wanting. Lies on the floor with books around her. All ears, questions. Pan of milk bubbling with cloves, the dance of letters heady in her. Singing is passable, psalms easy on her tongue. But she *will* sway with the force of them, lifting up, up onto her toes. Still goes to Cook for sweetness. Pears, raisins. Reads too quickly. The Earl says let her, anything for sweet Ælfgyva. She is hungry. Forgets to eat. Is hungry. Forgets.

●

Ælfgyva:

O long-leggéd spar hawk
    mantled over plunder, you dart away
                barrelling through the
        undergrowth and are gone
You leave me without
        guidance. Now! when the fat new
           pigeon of the bishopric
   has consecrated me to the task
        of Mother

        Doth the hawk fly by thy wisdom, stretch
        her wings toward the south?

Oh help me, come
    to your blackbird.
I dreamt you were fashioning
   feathers out of gold. My bones, strung
               on a necklace. But no
         the foundations
    of my heart are sound

Cusp and corbel – The choir & Ælfgyva

Comet in April and the Confessor dead   armies crisscross the island
The Bastard crosses the narrow sea   a ship built for him by his bride,
Matilda   On the Mora's greenwood prow, a gilded child   pointing
further   lips to a horn of ivory   The long boat tips William into
England   a little stumble then righted   With fists of sand, he claims
the shore   and with battle, the realm   Edyth, gentle swan, combs the
battlefield   Voices raised at the crowning   the welter of language
fires in Westminster and the congregation scattered   The new king
decamps to Barking   the Normans land like swans with heavy wings
they drop and skim, full of their own arrival

Choir:

Sweet Ælfgyva, mother of grace, scuffed knuckles. Still dreams
of a citadel on the river. Wants spires, wants windows. Taller by
a hand, she welcomes the conqueror. A gruff man of few graces.
Engages him on aspect, masonry, good quarries. He and his
queen have an abbey apiece, another planned as penance for all
the bloodshed. In broken French and signing, the abbess and the
king talk holy ribs and arches. While he receives the surrender of
the earls, she conceives a greater abbey. The pale stone of Caen
against the rag stone of Kent.

•

Ælfgyva:

Willelm Williame Guillaume, fresh from the coronation.
            Not much bother
    but good Lord he can eat.
            Off to Hainault for days of hunting.
       Returns hungry. He does not read.
  He loves to hear the sisters sing,
            Stay me with flagons, he hiccups

comfort me with apples.
                    The cook is at her wit's end.
Three months of him, as he rebuilds the Tower
            climbs the English sky in stone.
    Three months. My hospitality secures
        protection in return. He grants me
                    peace and love, and all the rights…
            à l'intérieur et l'extérieur
                        O watch me build!

                        •

Choir:

Years of battles, but by Ælfgyva's clever hand our new cloister
rises. *Where wast thou when I laid the foundation?* From afar you
can see the great abbey buttress the sky, hear the toil as men work
the walls. *Enlarge the place of your tent stretch your tent curtains
wide.* But now, long days of sighing – our impatient mistress.
Building stalled, and short of promised height. Her works stay
upon the church fathers. Tired of their must-not-overstep, tired
of their must-not-move-the-church, sweet Ælfgyva says, If I have
to lay the stones myself… Æthelburh has come to me this night
and said *Put my bones to work.*

                        •

Ælfgyva:

This Sabbath night, we approach the high
            white tomb. Our lanterns
    bob in the fog, the river, the chilly stone.
                    We crack the marble lids
                with iron. The offering of a pearl.
                The carved awning
        dances in devout procession. As light in the willows
                when the river stirs.

And here are caskets that brim
                    with milk-white bones and
          books! O what foresight to tell
                              of whom and where placed
                    so long ago.
We raise them from their beds of
          clay and sand, remove
      the relics to a temporary hall, singing
                    thou hast set my feet in a large room.

·

Choir:

Seven years while our Dido builds. Then one night, prostrate
in prayer and holy dust, by Æthelburh's tomb, the very slabs of
the crypt begin to shift. Sweet Ælfgyva pinned against the wall.
Short of breath she gasps, *My Lady please...*

·

Ælfgyva:

My Lady please, the force of you. I can hardly breathe.
                    But what is this?
                          From out the cold lodging
            of the crypt, a whirl
      of dust and flame, and my bright lady rising
                              saying, *Delay no more*
            re-house me somewhere fit.
O forgive, these slow bricks
                    for I have built, oh breath, a little house
                          for you, a crib.
            At this she smiles, releases me.
                                    Oh breath.
                    Steps free and is
      transformed. A little girl

she stretches out her arms. Pleads
Hold me,
in your bosom let me rest.
I feel the sweet milk prick
in my breast, gather her to me.
Devour me, I say, my milk
upon your chin.
I will be your fortress.

•

Choir.

So lullabies the ecstatic nurse, surrounded by the dead, their eerie psalms.

Sing O thou that didst not bear   break forth
aloud   thou that didst not travail with child

Settle down muddy beds – The washerwomen

At London, le couvre-feu   lights out at the sound of the evening peals
cold raked over hot, to stop   the city burning with conspiracies   Coals
of rebellion grumble till morn   Edith Forne, mistress of the king,
dreams of magpies   builds an abbey at Osney   A dove nests for
days in Beatrix's sleeve   and at Salisbury, the roof is blown clean off the
new cathedral   Houses demolished, sky wracked with seizures   a
convulsive child   Strength sufficient to hurl a cart, the great bridge of
the conqueror

THE GREAT WASH

At Winterfylleð we go down to the river. Bright day, a week
on from the feast of Æthelburh. Feast that covers the cook
in goose fat and gravy. Scrub, scrub her. Moon tonight will
be good for bleaching, will conspire with the white crisp of
the night. But first we gather. Take the baskets of soiled and
stale, the baskets of holy. Here comes the sexton with her
pot of saintly piss. We elbow each other, bite our saucy lips.

> Slip and slide on the reedy beds, settle down muddy
> bed we're not done yet.

Out to the river to full the clothes, to fling them and tread
them. Here where the stream elbows. Easy slip of the bed,
sward into gravel. Straight in is Thora with her joints crab
apple. Mean-fisted, swollen, blown by the river. Tough little
hands. Don't cross her, would work you like a dishcloth. Now,
would you look at the tits on the new girl! Thinks she's all
that, well the pike will have those. Holy Veronica, who does
she think? Gregory, set us a fire for when it gets too chilly.

> Slip and slide on the reedy beds, settle down muddy
> bed we're not done yet.

In the tub of linen, with a whisk of twigs. In the nostrils
– chamber lye, dissolved grease. The gall of a stubborn ox,
beaten into piss, rub with a fist of chicken feathers, squeeze
without twist. Gentle with the new veil. Saffron fringe, stiff
with gold floss acanthus. These good girls and their dirty
necks. Couldn't do their own. Imagine! Them out here up to
their dugs in wet. We walk through their underthings.

> Slip and slide on the reedy beds, settle down muddy
> bed we're not done yet.

Hours in the water, the mystery of our fingers. How they
swell, grow mazey with it. Woe betide the girl that lets the
river. A wrapper, lifted like a reed, then a fat elver. Better to
be swept after than tell the Missus. Learn quick to hold your
grip. White knuckles coaxing the river through a feast-day
shift. Bugger off, to the nose-bleeders.

> Slip and slide on the reedy beds, settle down muddy
> bed we're not done yet.

Cold hours crouched on the bank. Keep moving is the trick,
don't settle to it. Soapwort, neck grease and soupy bibs.
Sleeves trailed in ink. Their monthly tatters are a lost cause
but we freshen them nonetheless.

> Slip and slide on the reedy beds, settle down muddy
> bed we're not done yet.

THE DRYING

Away to the green, we wrap rocks in linen. Place them to hold
the wash. Dance with our nuns, each takes one. Unfold in a
reel across the bleaching field. Snap our partners in the sun,
shake out the river and bed them down. All the robes laid out,
without their bodies. The cellaresse a puzzle of old feast days,
breakfast.

Away to the green, wrap rocks in linen. Come frost,
come breeze, la lune.

Bring the children to run about, scare away the ducks, the
doves – their elderberry muck. The thieving crows. We
watch the weather, don't much like the look. Set a girl to
watch the fancy veils. Us, with our feet up.

Away to the green, wrap rocks in linen. Come frost,
come breeze, la lune.

THE STORM

We sit and watch the empty robes, the night watch over the
bleach field. To call for help if the wind gets up, if the sisters
start to move. We watch the altar coverlet, the chalice cloths.
But the day is long and, soon we're sleeping on the job.

We wake to a wall of dark and reaved with lightning. A
great and terrible wind. We run headless, gathering. Basket,
quick: throw in sisters Joan and Benedicta, chasuble and
cloak, make a bundle of the abbess. But the new veil! with
the fancy stitch, it gives us the slip.

Snatched by the squall from a lavender bush. It goes first to
swaddle a birch, then up to dust the hornbeams. We get our
fingers to a hem, but then, off again. Fingers to a hem. Run
till we are knotted up in leaf-stripped branches. Lifted off
our feet, returned. Lifted. As tripping down a step.

Above, two skies. One still and tacked with stars, the other
haste and racing. Dark green, tumbling debris. Balls of hail,
roaring. How does the heart? How does the heart hold to its
branch in such a brawling. We let go the laundry.

Up into the air, the howling. We gather the wind in our fists, move like storks above the estuary. Snuff up the wind, and are gone. Nothing but the whiff of lambswool.

Ink drawn from madder

— 12th century —

Red-capped – Adeliza

Century of signs and the sky folding, unfolding   red through apricot,
green   At sea, La Blanche-Nef   heavy with heirs   wrecked on
the Quillebœuf reef   Normandy, England, Anjou all robed in seaweed
And so the anarchy begins   The grief struck king declares for his one
remaining *Feme sole,* Matilda   England won't wear it   Trapped in
her winter castle, domina Anglorum   she darts in white across the Isis
escapes across the narrow sea   And so, king Stephen   For the support
of Barking, he gives them land upriver, grubs out trees   Adeliza builds
an infirmary for lepers   *causae et curae,* she makes them a bath

We heat the tub, stir in our courses, they go singing through the
water. Wring out the tatters, the bloody moss! The book says of
blood that therein lies the soul.

We bring them on with rue and wine. Hyssop. Hazelnut. Salve
medicina, therapeutic balm. Sticky, laboured. God has given us
this pain, it is god given. A garden where our flowers all spring at
once.

Red burnet and bloody dock. The blood in the holly at the heart
of the wood. As when the mouse piles up her hips and haws. As
when the fresh new bark of the birch.

The blood cries out, go in health, disease be gone. For the life of
the flesh is in the blood. From this watered soil let health, a tree
be borne. Thrust green, as when the virgin from whose chamber
grew the lord.

Stained night of ink drawn from madder, wake within a red
pavilion. The holy gate that gives and out comes a flood of copper.

Apron veined with garnet, ground cinnabar, the bib of the
fieldfare. As the brush, which tells its story in the wash. As when
a rose bush in Jericho fills the air.

I raise a cup, within which a flood. Pour onto the sickly ground, from which a slender tree begins to branch. Spring from the earth, well and sprightly! The green thrust of health, viriditas.

Red-capped, I am the green woodpecker of the lord.

Lark-tongued – Clémence

Epistles and visions cross the narrow sea   Hildegard, spoken of in cloisters everywhere Exuberant worship, symphonic whispers   gold crowns and unbound hair   Saladin takes Jerusalem, city of refugees and so the season of tithes begins   Each man shall give in alms, a tenth unless he joins the fray   the *pious* labour of pilgrimage   A force of thousands is raised   this land bereft of men and horses   A quarter of all income taken   Jews massacred at Bury, Lincoln   Ælred delivers a sermon for the Confessor   his Life translated at Barking into Anglo-Norman   When he dies, his skin is clearer than glass   brighter than garlic in the hedgerow

The swoop   the mirroring
    as when birds wheel   in the high anteroom
                    of the sky   turn from ink to silver
                            as they shift
          So our words   let them reach
    then flicker into brightness

When Catherine's wheel flew at her touch
               into a thousand pieces   everywhere
                   lodging   eloquent in the heart
Each splinter
        of light   a mirror of the mystery
                 we are each a mirror held to wonder
         each heart   each word cast out   glinting

And as the mirror does not lock up its light
             does not hold in some dark coffer   we will
       blast radiance into the world   increase
       the bright sparking
                a work of fire

And for the love of my sisters   this house
and for Catherine who was lark-tongued

                              I   Clémence   undertake this work
                  for who will speak for us
          if we do not   Our holy mother spoke
                                        in her own tongue
                    was fit to converse
                                        with angels   and to raise her son
          Did she lullaby that babe in some
                                ritualised tongue   She did not

To write is to reach beyond
                    not just the wonder of sound
                                        the ear   the heart
                    a common language for an uncommon tale
          the voice of then through the voice
                                of now
                    the language of *fin amor*
Dear heart   guide my pen
                          My name is Clémence   I say again

Men were not so clever then, nor so envious
as they are now – Mary Becket | Marie de France

Henry moves Eleanor from one grim fortress to the next   No more the
court d'amour   Sometimes summoned to the palace, and then   queen
consort of England again   Nothing to read but the stars above the castle
She dreams of her library, her buckskin gloves   the weight of a hawk
through her forearm   To atone for the death in the cathedral, Becket's
sister is made abbess at Barking   to be put aside when the king's natural
daughter comes of age   Each day more pilgrims   holy ampoules,
miracles of recovery   Eleanor, now queen dowager, raises a ransom for
her son   the swaggering red king   The pile grows in the vault of St
Paul's, the dragon of famine, poverty   The poor are tumbled into beds
of earth   blood-soaked soil below the gallows

So this is Berkyng, lord the smell! We are
brought to a river, reeking and deep. Come horse,
step carefully through this busy place.

I shall be glad to meet with Clémence, and yet
I fear her. Will this veil strike the right note?
Should I enter the blessed gate on horseback

or on foot? Well, I suppose, if I am to be abbess…
Oh, there is expediency in this, me
a means to affirm the king's innocence

in your death. Brother, he vows, of your blood
his hands are clean. You, his troublesome priest.
They say he is not my enemy. And anyhow,

where else would the world have me be?
I cannot go to Agnes, nor Rose. They have
their own sore hearts to nurse. I will not marry.

You are loved, and people know I am your sister.
When we crossed Matilda's bridge at Bow
there were reverent people out to watch us.

I am to them a vial, through which drifts a drop
of you. A thousand vials of Catherine's balm
could not restore you. An abbey for a saint though.

I will be as much a draw here as the rood.
When my fingers cramp with chills there will be fire
to release my verse. But what of the words

that do not come, and have not since you
were killed. Will this hearth release them?

·

Oh the freedom of solitude! To think,
to breathe. No more the snagging of the brain,
the thorns of some empty ditty. To dip

my pen into a finer ink. A different horse,
a terrain of peace. Stirrups of psalm
and this quill for a crop. Saddle cloths

sewn with the Becket choughs. And what
a house this is! A high buzz of wisdom, wit.
Even the novices are here *scholares*.

Saint Benedict bade us read, but surely
urges with his own name: speak.
Speak well he says, and truly this is

a house of silver tongues, tolled for
goodness and the word. Do we not read
each time we write? Is the Rule not thus

fulfilled? At least, such is my thinking.
I'll not be listless, an idle soul, *ora et labora*.
Clémence has her Catherine. For me, La vie

Seinte Audree. I'll not shirk my tongue.
I will sing of her dew-sprinkled innocence
cloaked in a wedding veil, her place

at the eternal court of heaven. Gold, tempered
in tribulation. Her isle of eels, her ash tree.

•

Such comfort in the rhythm of our days,
the structure of the Hours, the space.
The stable of my desk, the slanted reed.

There is work, but also time to ride the word.
We journey far within these walls, this
paddock of hay and prayer. There are hedges,

we spur each other on and over. Riders,
unassailed. To not hold back, to give it all
instead, the very moment that one has it.

Unbridled! And yet, I am still busy with
your pilgrims, Brother. Most recently
Guernes. He has lost his manuscript, his Vie

St Thomas, and so comes to me. I remain
your faithful keeper. I gave him a fine horse,
a generous welcome. And today, he writes

it was a fair throw of the dice that sent him
to my house, promises he will sing my praises
to all he meets. *Great and small* he says. Perhaps…

But she who forgets herself is foolish. I write
my name, Marie, that I be not forgotten.

The innocents

— 13th century —

Massacre of the innocents – Christiana de Valoniis

At odds with the king, the pope places the country under orders   for years, only baptism and absolution   a quiet grows in the church   The king starves Moll Walbee, legends grow   She is an ogre with an apron of stones, who eats her own   The king retreats across the Marches, loses his crown jewels   wagons caught by tide on the causeway   quicksand and holy marsh   A dish of peaches finally carries him off   At Barking, a great doom is painted on the chancel arch   gluttony riding a panther tail in one hand, flagon in the other

A riot of small feet, as our exalted schoolgirls practice the Mystery in the alleys of the nave. We grant them revelry, indulgencies. Oh, much missed Childermastide!

They skid down the church in a peal of giggles. Little Maud elected to upside-down my dignity. *For he hath put down the mighty from their seat.* She has me perfectly.

My seal of office is too heavy for her fingers, she makes do with bulrushes. Our sweet Abbess of Fools, in her fustian and veil, embroidered by the prioress.

Her motley choir twit-twoos the psalms. Disguises, masks. They fly and hoot around the cloister, then rush towards the kitchen demanding rissoles.

Maud brings a seriousness to the role of fool. Out with her school-girls, levying donations, she is unrefusable. The lark and dance is a brightness, it brings the Unrule.

Sombre at the feast she bids us
remember the children, this day
of massacre. Rachel and her sisters
pleading for their boys. The little
tumbled bodies, the pitiless king.

Menagerie – Maud de Leveland

The boy-king is crowned in a modest chaplet   He is fond of shrines,
marries Eleanor   She is twelve, already unpopular   A doting bride
in gold and ermine   she cannot get enough of books   They name
their first son for the Confessor   Henry signs a charter for the forest,
restores the commons   A bright star stands in the sky for days   He
rebuilds Edward's shrine, plants a forest of tapers   Spends and spends
And then, new laws   voices to be lowered in synagogues   a wearing
of badges, two pieces of yellow   no more the wet-nursing of Jewish
children   Homes are sacked, there is burning   Canterbury, Derby
coins in the well at Lincoln   When Henry dies, they lay him to rest in
the saint's old coffin

We are summoned by Eleanor,
who wishes to be a patron of the
abbey. She greets us in red damask
and a silver girdle, in which, a
conspicuous dagger. She wears a
flamboyant wimple.

She is delighted by our gift of
Aesop, takes us first to the lions. I
tell her they look like the old king,
am old enough to remember. Their
long faces and tawny hair, their
lean yet apathetic hunger.

They prowl their small cells, swag
and twist as they turn. Have
grown to loathe each other, the
way they mirror. Don't watch me
eat this spoonful of meat. The way
they bare the cages of their teeth.

She says they call the snow bear
Hearken, after the king of Norway
whose gift he was. He is like a great
white dog, allowed out of the Tower

He bewilders the light, it scatters through him. The spray as he careens, great paws in the shale and mud of the shore. His keeper tames him with a strange-tongued song, but I think it is the song of cruelty. He stares disconsolate, upriver.

They have built him a long room where they make him do tricks. His voice carries all the way to Berkyng. Bells have nothing on that strange hosanna, his trunk a bell rope swinging. Truly, *in whose hand the soul of every living thing?*

on a very stout rope. He swims in the Thames, which heaves with cormorants and careless fishermen.

The giant was ridden all the way here like a broad grey mare. Tall enough to walk the narrow sea. He loves to squirt and flounder. All London out to see the horned-moons of his teeth. He is like a fond uncle, his soft pink tongue and grin. He is kept well on wine and beef.

Enclosure – Alice de Merton

The tall king comes to power   an earthquake at Glastonbury   Year-on-year, the weather changing   Storms and floods, the Thames encroaching surges, inundation   St Lucy redraws the coastline   hundreds are lost Longshanks orders an extermination   all the wolves in England   Woods are burned to the ground coppicing to drive them out   Six hundred Jews imprisoned at the tower, the long room of the elephant Hundreds hanged, it takes months Finally expulsion   all to be gone by All Hallows   Four pence for passage to France, two for the poor   families left to drown on the sandbanks of Sheppey   bodies washed up on the shore

Ottobon and Peckham drum a storm of regulations, minute and particular: our feast of the innocents to be conducted *with decency, in private; lest the divine praise become a mockery; lest by repeated intercourse, the quiet and contemplation; confessor, doctor, father, brother; always have with her the elder, wiser members of the house, nuns above suspicion; only for causes necessary, inevitable; forbidden, all visits for pleasure; except seriously, and in a public place; except for evident advantage, or urgent necessity; never to leave it, except for fit cause and in company; punctually, so that chatter may cease; no one to go into the parlour after sunset; to hold our processions here only, the confines of this house; places beyond those specified, entirely forbidden; wine for the altar shall not be sour.*

I must, must not remain
in my room, *Selah.*

Three hundred oaks

— 14th century —

The great famine – Anne de Vere

Robert and Elizabeth are crowned in defiance of the English   She tells
him, *I am but queen of the may and you my garland king*   Edward goes
to France for a bride   requests carts, horses   The royal privy balanced
on Barking's fish cart, bobbing across the sea   The Scottish campaign
grumbles in the belly of England   Barking ordered to send victuals
Edward sends them the captured may queen   Anne writes   *he thinks
we are his prison, his granary*   The rain that will not end for years begins
Crops fail and in time there is famine

We are sent a pensioner
      of the king's stable, to ensure his maintenance
                              for life. But life is short, and he comes to us
                  on a pale horse. Even the Bishop
      sends his girls for us to feed. This is a slow
            and winding dance.

We trap rabbit, fox and badger. Cat and vermin.
                              The salt men cannot
                  evaporate brine, this weather, and so the meat
does not last. We have a little grain
                              from the king, but the people have
                  none. They eat like deer
            roots, grasses, bark.

The country is become a place of veils.
                  All is marsh, a pasture of rain.
No dry austerities, instead the continuous falling,
                              and the river lifting. The terrible folds
            of the cattle, lowing after
                  remembered cud.

Rain with its message of refreshment
            that stands and stands continually replenishing,
                              as mouths spool into years.
            No more the gold of wheat

to be spun into loaves, no green cud spun
into fat and meat.

The people, exist like linnets,
dandelion, groundsel, lichen.
Long since slaughtered, the Martinmas ox,
the seed stock
eaten.

The children are like kites of sticks
slack pennants, no breath in them
only rain.
We find them in the woods,
poor babes, hunger stopped with clay.
We keep as many here as we can,
we are godmothers to twigs.

Try to keep our strength.
We dwindle and share.

Sisters Dulcie and Desiderata
exist on the Eucharist.
That spare wafer, a little vinegar.

The grapes have failed, the granaries are
desolate. This Lenten year that will not end.
We turn in, and in.
The hard grate of hunger. There is a book, there is.
A little porridge. The dust of the mill.

I pass my keys to Sister Eleanor
for the day of his wrath is come
and who shall be able to stand?

Morsel – Sister Dulcie

In Paris, a trial for heresy   the wandering beguine, Marguerite Porete
The ash of her *pestiferous* book   the Mirror of Simple Souls   drifts
through Europe   The inquisitor declares her a *fake woman*   she becomes
her own annihilated soul   It ends at the stake   Rough-sawn timber
faggots and straw

Holy nothing, round as a mirror
I am nothing
blasted to nothing
marrow
thin as a panel beaten till the light
my shoulders lit
light in my fingers
I'll eat nothing but the Eucharist
feast on spirit
glow with the winnowing
this little crisp that sits
in the pool of my tongue
it fills me
how the saliva rushes to meet it
salve!
to dissolve into honey
sweet morsel
my body is meat
a loaf to be crumbled
do not summon me with that old name
I am honey and I am grain
a nameless feast
to fall famished from love
into nothingness
and bliss

Three hundred oaks – The woodsman's wife

The abbey falls into disrepair   Eleanor petitions the king, who grants
a felling   Three hundred oaks, to roof and buttress   if she can find
the men   How to haul the heart out of the wood with all the draught
animals long slaughtered   But slowly the granary sings again   dry grain
a roof over the rectory

The boy wants to watch his father work so
we go with the woodsmen Lucky to have a
boy they tell me so many lost to the famine
But the nuns kept him in scraps god love
them Those days of next-to-nothing then
nothing-at-all No end to this forest and my
feet fair sore The boy high on his shoulder
all ears for the axe the voice of his father
hard and good for splitting He tells him the
woods *the oak, its great green coat the beech
that slings off its branches this hornbeam
this elm* This was how he caught me my
Jack of the green *oak galls for the abbey ash
sap for my babes* I go giddy for looking
and looking then *Look!* I show him *Up
there mistletoe! It's a blessing* We'll bring a
garland for every girl in the village make
them fat again and sticky The boy runs
around pretending *chock, chock, chock* the
song of the chopping His daddy brings
him a nest a tiny coracle His sister could've
curled up in it

The great pestilence – Maud Montagu (elder)

The king sends his daughter Joan to marry Spain   She departs from
England's shore in green silk sewn with wild men and roses   She has
a hundred bowman and a portable chapel   stitched with dragons   A
whole ship for her dowry alone   Her wedding dress is the length of an
abbey   spun with gold, low sun reaching across water   But she never
wears it   Her bowmen cannot save her from this new adversary   she dies
at Bordeaux   And so the great pestilence announces   I will have you,
high and low   your rags   your enamelled buttons

Dark nights when the grim barges
set off from London to ease their horrid cargo
into marsh.

The boneyards are full and there is a foulness
so they nose their blue prows into reed
then tip them out.

But the tide brings the bodies. They lift and bloat
in pasture. With long staves, our men push them
back out into the water

and the brown Thames bears them away,
its long and winding grief. Go, Christian souls
out of this world.

Go, in the name of the Father that made thee
from nought, leave this unlovely marsh.
So many priests,

they take Mass, and then are taken. This one
barely knows the viaticum, has not
the craft of dying.

There is a strange mood of morbidity
among the living. New laws against idling,
a cap on wages.

And in every town, we must build stocks.
Merchants, vagrants, lepers, alike are hounded.
Our hospital gives me pause.

There has been a great combustion, a star
that haunts the sky for days. There is
a loneliness in this.

Apples, hard and purple, grow in the soft curves
of the body. But our Lady succours us
in anguish.

I wrap myself fully in His death, that my soul fall
never downwards. Grant that my last hour be my best.
In manus tuas domine…

The harrowing of hell – Katherine de Sutton

A great storm tide, whole parishes swallowed in the drowning   The
plague comes again, this time for the children   the Pestilence of Boys
Catherine of Siena weds the Son, his foreskin around her finger   The
grass grows high in the streets   *A little thing, the size of a hazelnut,* the
visions of Julian of Norwich   Alice Perrers, daughter of a thatcher, is
mistress to the king   Lady of the Sun, she parades in gold around the
city   Harlot, they say   she rules the country   Laws drafted against
her, all women   The corn dolly ploughed back into the land   Katherine
provides a good ash for the maypole   She builds a curfew tower, moves
the rood screen   Abbey lands are underwater   she coerces labour
Wallis et fossatis   sea walls, dykes

Draft of a letter from Katherine de Sutton
to Sibyl Aucher of Wilton –

I am sorry for your difficulties: the burden of corrodies, your
daughters given to superstitious games, etcetera. Here too at
Berkyng, there was an ennui. But the soul's vitality demands we
resist. Lest through sloth & sluggardy, the devil ensnare. And so,
new plays for Holy Week. Cecilia has a gift for drama. Her busy
choir, the bright clouds of their breath, o chilly spring. The goodly
chores of preparation. Embroidery, costume, prop, etcetera.

For the taking down of the cross, *above all woods of cedars you
alone excel,* a role for our taller priests. I have them wash it in
wine and water, then lay it in woollen & white linen. A niche,
well scrubbed of dust & before which, a candle. Then on Holy
Saturday, ad infernos! To greater engage the congregation, I have
moved the *elevatio* hard on the heels of the Harrowing.

Our new procession, as follows. The convent, plus certain clerics
are together in the small chapel. Palms & unlit candles, waxy as the
dead. And hung on the chapel door, a hell mouth. Stupendous &
yawning, lips drawn into a sneer. Terrible of aspect, pale Disease

& Hunger are there. And Strife, a bloody ribbon in his uncut hair. Much fun & pricked fingers in its preparation.

For the *descensus*, I have added dialogues. Christ sings *Tollite portas* thrice in a rising voice, striking with his staff, the very mouth. Like thunder *Open up and let my people pass.* And we, the brides of Christ play patriarchs & prophets. Four thousand six hundred years have we dwelt, grinding our teeth in flaming fire. Gathered in the dark, we sing for our soul's release. Wailing, piteous & hopeful.

> *From the gate of hell*   *O Lord rescue my soul*
> *Lord rescue me*   *From hell*

At the third strike, the hell mouth opens. Eve pleading the light not turn from her. *Et ne declines in ira ab ancilla tua!* Do not shun your handmaid. And there, dread Belsabub, who calls out *Burst are all our bands of brass!*

Then we patriarchs proceed. Woe to well, & bale to bliss, out into the bright lit church. Smoke & solemn instruments, a priest who swings the censer well. Lastly, the visit to the sepulchre, a further change. It is absurd that the three Marys be played by men. Our three chosen sisters dress in egg-white surplices. Then, heads covered with shining veils, they confess and I absolve them. The three proceed, saying *Eheu! Misere! Such harrowe! Who moved the stone?* and suchlike. By turns tearful and subdued, plaintive, joyful. Sighing and due solemnity. And at the tomb? Can a sister be an angel? I think she can. Nay, we had two. Sabine, who you know, and dear sister Olive, *Mulier quid ploras?! Why do you look for the living among the dead?*

If you wish, can send manuscripts forthwith…

The worth of a penny – Maud Montagu (younger)

The boy marries Anne of Bohemia   A long-haired comet in the sky Fern
and ostrich, she brings no fortune   When she arrives at London, her
ships smash into kindling   Little scrap of a thing, she can barely manage
her wedding crown   emerald, pearl, ruby, sapphire   her head blazes for
days   The love-struck teens tour the realm   Barking unreachable due
to flooding   Anne is kind to the pregnant, to widows   intercedes   on
behalf of London   She dies at Sheen from the pestilence   grief struck,
the king burns it to the ground

No one to plough, and the worth of a penny
in chaos. The town quay, the dredging
of the Roding, broad river walks to protect
our grazing. All to be paid for. Lay pockets
are emptied by the crown, their wars, their
pageantry. Three poll taxes in as many years.
This is an ungodly parliament. Outrages
of proof, twelve pence for anyone with hair
on their body. The sheriffs brand those
who will not pay, an f on the forehead. It is
unchristian. At the new king's privilege,
another mouth to feed, Chaucer's daughter
joins us. Perhaps she will have her father's pen.
The younger sisters call her Chaucy, *the little
slipper*. The king's uncle, endows us richly,
he is her godfather. It is something, but will not
repair the flood walls. He speaks well of
Wycliffe, his damning of clerics, their excesses.
Present company, he says, *excepted.*

Wycliffe's cadre of poor fathers move like a great rumour through the land
the wealth of the church, the witchcraft of transubstantiation The priest
of England's village green addresses the people   *Choose liberty! Cast off
the yoke!*   Women incarcerated for raising their voices Catherine of

Siena travels freely, writes letters urging reform *God is a sea, in which we are fish* She is buried above a temple to an older goddess her severed head, a bag of rose petals At Blackfriars, an earthquake troubles the synod

The Thames and Roding conspire, breach
and storm tide turn us into farmers of fish.
I raise a town of shipwrights. Wives, good
with a kiddle: wattled stakes, for which
I allow timber. They stretch in rows from
shore to low water, clever baskets in the middle.
Banned by the great charter, but these are days
of extraordinary need. With whom do I hold?
With King Richard and the true commons,
as is whispered. He exempts us from muster,
knows our reserves are gone to thrusting back
the water. The rivers take and they give, steal my
usable pasture but give me fish. There is a power
in this. For she who commands the mouth
of the river can feed her people. When surveyors
come from the city, they say they are attacked,
armed groups shouting *Hence, traitors!* I say,
I cannot speak to that. A lake has formed
about the breach and the marsh is lost.
It is perilous for ships, but our lads are adept.

A great burning of papers, a throwing open of the gaols women abroad with staves and sticks, their voices Debt records scattered on the wind The beldam Margery, she yells *Away with the learning of clerks, away with it* The commons come singing across a heath of clover, nonesuch, vetch splashed milk, scooped butter The young king meets them at Smithfield orders a charter of freedom Ferrour marches on Gaunt, tips his wealth into the Thames *We are not robbers!* She levels his palace, orders executions *for the commons do not love them* Heads marched through Essex strangers dragged from churches The gory block of rebellion, the axe with two edges

When the kings of the earth take tribute
it falls heavy on the poor. People resist
the poll tax, seek an end to unpaid labour.
The preaching of John Ball ignites all Essex.
The sheriff's home looted, torched. We hear
of riots in Cambridge, attacks on priests.
The prior at Bury, beheaded. At odds with
the old and in hope of better, they rebel.
But this violence, I cannot bear. I counsel
peace. My heart aches for the powerless,
I have seen violence. Watched my father,
and his men (be sure I do not forget you)
beat my mother to death, *their full weight
and weapons*. Heroes of Crécy. My sister
in my arms as they went at it, no son to mould
into another bully. Murderous, without pity.
I am the last of his blood, his line will die
with me. It is a blessing, but so will hers
which is a sin. She was of Norfolk, her name
was Alice. Her murderers were pardoned
by a king. And this king, my cousin, spits on
his own promises, crushes rebellion, says
serfs you are and serfs you shall remain.

Books and cellars

— 15th century —

Mustard, and salt biscuits – The cellaress

Kiddle riots and high tides   sweeping over the walls of the river   The
weather runs amok   Hundreds of acres lost to the breach at Barking   a
boat forfeit to the king, its use by pirates   Roaring Margery   mother
of fourteen   miller, mystic   dictates a book to her confessor   Her life,
the grief and graft of it, threatened with the stake for preaching   The
dowager's sons by Owen Tudor cost Barking a fortune   retinues and
tutors, the slow exchequer   They are grateful for the rood loft and the
dispensation   divine offices, food on the table   Fish wash up on the
marshes, they are fed to livestock

I dream of eel &
herring Stockfish
Weights & measures
plague me in my sleep
Talk in the market of
dabs & flounders
wicker traps &
fishwives Loaves &
fishes Our oaks are
gone to Henry Fewer
acorns for our hogs
Each lady shall have a
livery – one cheek /
one ear / one foot
makes one The groin
/ two feet – another
My head awash with
numbers

The vicar is to have nothing
to do with any
of the sisters   on pain of his
exclusion from our table
I suffer no thing
to go to waste   though it be
of little value I send to Smithfield
& Saint Albans   oatmeal / malt &
milk Watch my cooks & clerks   my
rent gatherers The bake house
the brew house   the buttery & kitchen
The making & mowing
of hay   the hiring
of pasture

I shall slay but every
fortnight & be a good housewife
beef three times a week   In Lent
to every lady – two pounds of
almonds / a half of rice
a pound of figs & raisins
Double to the prioress   myself &
to the kitchener   There must be
crumb-cakes / fritters / chicken / geese
Ale / spiced pies & wine
And marybones to make white worties
Borage / violet / mallow
Also parsley / flour & almond milk /
saffron / salt & honey

For Shrovetide – crisps & cakes
fat conies   Stub-eels /
shaft-eels to bake on Maundy
wheat & milk for frumenty
Gallons of red for the convent /
a pottle of Tyre for the abbess
Half a goose each
at Assumption / twelve hundred
red herring at
Advent   And when the toil
of Autumn has ceased
– the butchery & salting –
bonfires / lanterns
And on certain days
a pittance

Celeresse of the Monestarij of Barkynge

Hic liber constat – Sister Julian

Christine lives by her pen she builds a citadel of ladies Saints and virgins
warriors, sibyls An unlettered maid in breeches leads an army against the
English *feeds France with the sweet milk of peace* Joan belts and buckles
herself in, a skirt no protection The heresy of cross-dressing They burn
her three times, her ashes tipped into the Seine the river carries her to the
narrow sea Christine's song of her reaches Barking

Certayne bookes yn the Abbey of
Barkynge

Lives of the saints & desert
fathers, black leather without
boards : Goscelin's Lives of the
mothers – Ethelburga, Hildelith,
Edith, Hildebert of Lavardin : a
metrical life of St Mary : Ælred
of Rievaulx's Life of St Edward
the Confessor in lattyn, inscr.
*Quem qui celaverit vel fraudem de
eo fecerit anathema sit* : translation
of Ælred of Rievaulx's Life of St
Edward in Anglo-Norman : Sister
Clemence's Life of Catherine,
vernacular : Lives of Christiana,
Radegunde, Elfgiva : La Vie Seinte
Audree, in the hand of Marie, a
copy also of L'espurgatoire Seint
Patriz – vernacular : various tracts,
sermons & meditations : the bible
in englisshe, especially licensed,
with gold initials : a psalter & a
boke of hours : a Song of Songs
– dark red leather, inscr. *Hic est
liber sancte Barkynge* : a large

hymnary, with music : prayers &
meditations, calendars : a great
mass – white leather, clasp broken
: ~~Porete's Mirror, clasped with
gilt, silver – in Flemish~~ : a mirror
of the life of Christ, inscr. *Thys
bouke belongyth to [unreadable]*
: Hildegarde of Bingen, Scivias
transl. : the chart of our
cellaress : ordinale & customary,
Sibille de Feltoun, eyes of abbess
only : notes on the ringing of
bells – anonymous : liturgical
gospels (Jerome & Eusebius in
margin), large & bound in red
leather, clasped with brass : works
devotional & moral – French :
Le livre de la citee des dames,
white leather, tasselled with
green silk, clasped with silver –
Pizan, also her Ditie de Jehanne
d'Arc, illuminated : legends &
fabels, both Issop & Golden :
tracts on the cleansing of souls,
ethics, doctrine, ~~Bald's leechbook
& miscellaneous remedies~~ :
Canterbury Tales, with legend :

Wycliffe's Sussana, Magnificat & Benedictus in uno volumine – heretical, keep under key : prayers in lattyn & englisshe – inscribed in red : Liber Scintillarium, boke of sparks – Defensor : the Easter plays of Katherine de Sutton : a cronicle of England, tooled red goatskin : Artistotle's Ethica, Virgil's Aeneid & Cicero's Obligations, cum commento : letters – Osbert to his nieces, ~~Aldhelm to Hildegard~~ ~~(lost)~~, Goscelin to Elfgiva : Augustine's Lamentations, with gloss : Liber feretrariorum Sancti Æthelburge, inscr *hic est liber beate Aethelburge uirginis Berkingensis ecclesie* chained in the sacristy

Dolls of lead – Katherine de la Pole

Cobham glitters through London   the throne, a stone's throw for her
and Gloucester   She needs the buckle of an heir, a poppet of her own
obtains the necessary herbs   philtre of pig liver, the stones of a hare to be
drunk as the tide comes in   But as the river rises, so does it sink Accused
of necromancy   designs against the king   she is made to walk barefoot
through the city   the crowd given free rein   Margery Jourdemayne is
burnt at Smithfield   Margaret of Anjou marries the mad king   London
takes to the rooftops, no one can move for pageantry   In the war of the two
houses she finds the *heart and belly of a man*   but Lancashire falls to
York in a snowstorm   the bloody meadow, the beck that runs red for
days   Jacquetta escapes the Kingmaker, his charge of witchcraft   the
use of hearsay to accuse her   dolls of lead, broken and bound with wire

So much intrigue and squabble
    we hear of it
    of course
London only a day's ride
    through forest
    it grows ever closer
Less and less
    this life
    of contemplation
Father forgive me
    for I love these books
So hard to sit
    for more than
    half the hour
The business
    of this office
I hear from Alyce
    that Gloucester has gifted
    two hundred books
    to Oxford
Forgive my

jealousy
There is
         this intrigue
         of his flamboyant wife
         against the king
Talk of wax, black masses
         her soothsayer Jordameyne
Eleanor pleads
         only to charms
         to secure
         a child
Alyce says I should
         look to the abbey
         that no one be
         permitted
         to read our herbals
And now my brother
         has placed Gloucester
         so popular with
         the commons
         under house arrest
Oh William
         the king holds you
         in his heart, but daily
         you add to
         your unpopularity
I fear it will go hard
         for me and for
         your good wife
         Alyce

A barge arrives at Queenhythe   spring-felled oak and beech, stakes for
the Lollards   Wyche is burned at Tower Hill   the vicar at All Hallows-in-
Barking mixes sweet spice with his ashes, he is arrested   To deter pilgrims
the site is turned into a dunghill   Bloody battles on the bridge over the
Thames, Cade's rebellion   Katherine's brother is tried at sea, beheaded

His body on the sands at Dover   She reconstructs the curfew tower, a
new bell in the rood loft   The king designates their church at All Hallows
a chantry for the beheaded

Poor Alyce
    like St Anne
    she has now survived
    three husbands
This last
    my brother
She gives herself
    this time
    to widowhood
    and beads
Her library
    a comfort
She remains
    a Chaucer, subtle
    and canny
Enough to steward
    that vast estate
A woman with a mind
    is fit for any task
    she is fond of
    quoting
I can see her
    in her library
    the tapestry wall
St Anne teaching
    the Virgin
    to read
Our discussions
    of Pizan, who
    knew her father
Her copy of *La cité*
    des dames

She sends me a book
     of William's
The pages flare
     it was his favourite
If I hold it to my face
     I can perhaps
     smell him
His fingers have rubbed
     this page with
     his slow reading
The brass buckle
     replaced from
     clumsy use
When I am gone
     will my successor
     some sister
     of the future
     lift my books to her face
     and find me
     in them
This page thumbed
     this one
     a little sooty
The way this other
     falls open

Tender mothers – The choir

The protector of the realm accuses Elizabeth Shore   messages, sorcery
She escapes with penance in her petticoats, the crowd moved to pity   *A
proper wit had she, neither mute nor ful of bable*   In Rome, Innocent's bull
regarding sorcery   creaks open a door, through which steps the Hammer
of Witches   Old girls are said to suckle the devil   stop, for spite, the
milk in cattle   Innocent, thin and on his deathbed, drinks only the milk
of tender mothers

From the seed of the hawthorn comes
the may, the comb flowing with honey.
O maiden who bears the word without seed,
gifts flow from you, sweet basin of the holy.
Water ever-flowing through the never-opening
doorway. Watered pasture, star not falling.
Balsam, myrtle, olive. The well by the gate
that slakes all thirsting, amber jug outpouring.
Nourish me at your lovely breast, swaddled
in your wings of grace. Queenly balm for snare
and sorrow, font of oil, o jar of perfume.
Light filled with light, your inner chamber,
breast, from which floods milk and nectar.
O sweet, no jar of bitter, rose and violet,
honeysuckle. O queen of lilies you are river,
bank and harbour, all my solace.

The last abbess

— 16th century —

If not for her sex, she could have defied
– Thomasina Jenney

Red hair tumbling to promising hips   the midsummer crowning
of the rose and pomegranate   Katherine bears three boys, sickly or
still   the first stays for bells, beacons John the Black Trumpet in his
green-gold turban Katherine leads the army, heavy with child   it is a
warm September In time, a daughter   colicky, tenacious   The work of
annulment begins Catalina, mistress of the bedchamber   the intimacies
of linen   A falcon lands on the king's wrist, *whereon to rest, and buld her*
nest   Anne is clever, witty *gentill burd, as white as curd,* goes the ballad
She is crowned with the crown of kings for the boy they hope is in her
Cornhill hung with red arras, tissue, gold   She gives birth to a girl   Her
craving for apples, two boys that do not stick   another wife unpicked
Then Jane, good with a needle   gives him a guzzling boy   she dies post
partum, her cravings for quail

List of effects— Bedspreads & banners opus Anglicanum
Things broidered in-house or at Arras Receipts tendered
Cutter lane, London Items of ambivalent meaning to Greenwich
others for destruction Gold thread & other metal pearls
etcetera to be recovered A great cloth of red powdered w.
butterflies   several sisters hard at their desk *So our words let*
them reach then flicker into brightness Large coverlet of blue &
better blue faded at one edge Doves, geese an abbey rising
Altar frontals of green damask powdered w. woodbine, roses
pomegranate Banner of blue silk broidered length to height
Bold comet standing & a great sheet of light Female figure
in silver gold cords w. underside couching Rich coverlet of
green velvet bright lights in the sky scrollwork, blossom
Vestment of black damask w. roses & stars Figures,
one of which w. fingers *bright as with comets* White curtain
w. edging of trewlyps & bluebells St Anne & the Virgin bent
over letters Nun lifting with the jump of a bell rope Humorous,
in linen Large coverlet of lily flowers *Audrey me fecit*
Coverlet of green w. birch trees, river Large door-hanging

on which a hellmouth *Tollite portas!* only tolerably stitched
Coverlet of white & blue roses Saint Dorothea, perhaps Pomona
in orchard   crown of fruit & flowers Coverlet of red &
white w. trellis & birds Before a small chapel caskets of bones,
books *to tell of whom and where placed so long ago* Hanging,
in red w. daisy-chain of girls faces in split-stitch, worked
in spirals Single word, *scholares* silk Elaborate cope
showing martyrdom a breaking wheel, a book Another w.
scenes from the Assumption billows, small angels in seed
pearls Thirty plain winter cloaks good lambswool
Much bed linen and miscellaneous pillows

Unceasing choir – Dorothy Barley

Vives urges the learning of maids   they should study wisdom, but hold
their tongues demurely   Mothers who rely on wet nurses should avoid
those who chatter Margaret More translates Erasmus   her own voice
lifting off the page   Across the country, voices raised against enclosure,
dissolution   For her part in the pilgrimage of grace, Margaret Cheyne is
burnt at the stake   Barking must provide timber for battleships   Henry
as profligate with boats as with his masses   And so ends nine hundred
winters   in a tearing down of flint   The abbey swept away as with
brushwood   Only the curfew, the river   the unceasing choir of midges
Dorothy swears   *diligently I shal be attendant unto the kynges nedes*

Now for women   earthly marriage
                the only option
                        to win   without serious word   a husband
Show no token of mis-order
                        mild conversation
Henry has put off
                two queens   both of whom prized learning
                        gave him hearty daughters
He has sent his assessors here   they know the worth of
                everything   and nothing
                        They will find no crass bundles
                                miraculous wimples
        no girdles for peasant girls   We are not
                        a *suspicious mansion*
I am to surrender to Petre   a man
                to whose daughter
                        I am friend and godmother
        she bears my name
Her father is a man sprung from Æsop's willow
                he will bend and help
                        himself
                                to our books   their bindings
        Our walls   we are reduced to assets

                    stones   intended for
                              busy palaces   highways
                                   Good bricks
                         to be taken to the wharf
The men with chisels come
          and the men with statutes
                              we shall not live together
                              in more than three or four
          we shall not leave together
          on pilgrimage   nor be given any alms
                         we shall   we shall not   marry
                              we shall return to society
                    we who are   accustomed
          to our own
No more library   or quiet worship
          the field of letters
                    No more the interruption of
                         the schoolgirls   *the vigour*
                                   of the sweet apple
                    The books of our foremothers
                              to be handled by strangers
                    No more the quiet arches
                    and scriptorium
          to sit with one book   one thought
          for months on end
          to climb in it   as a child within a tree
                    Our orchard   unprotected
                         its walls stoved in
And so I will not die in office
                    If this chapbook comes into your hand
                         know this
          I was the last abbess of a great house
                    I was not noble
          so will not be known   but I
                         Dorothy Barley
                         Abbatissa de Berkyng
          undid   was made to undo this

Dissolution | the scattering of the beads

Elizabeth Badcok ∞ Margery Ballard ∞ Elizabeth Banbrik
∞ Dorothy Barley ∞ Margaret Bramston ∞ Agnes
Buknam ∞ Margaret Cotton ∞ Joan Drurye ∞ Martha
Fabyan ∞ Dorothy Fitzlewes ∞ Joan Fyncham ∞ Matilda
Gravell ∞ Margaret Grenehyll ∞ Agnes Horsey ∞ Alice
Hyde ∞ Thomasina Jenney ∞ Margaret Kempe ∞
Lucy Long ∞ Audrey Mordaunt ∞ Winifred Mordaunt ∞
Margery Paston ∞ Katharine Pollard ∞ Elizabeth Prist ∞
Margaret Scrowpe ∞ Gabriel Shelton ∞ Anne Snowe
∞ Suzanna Suliarde ∞ Agnes Townesend ∞ Mary Tyrell
∞ Ursula Wentworth ∞ Elizabeth Wyott ∞

Epilogue

As when a great oak is taken down, its limbs divided and sent to diverse places. Some go to the dockyard to become a great ship, and some to become rough tableware. Some go to become the boards about a book. Some wheels, some caskets. And some go to be consumed by fire. Yet still, each holds within it the leaf, the acorn, the yellow rosary of the catkin. And the limbs are gone as relics about the land, and one goes here, another there. And others, where the wasp has been, are gone to ink.

Timeline

Characters

Notes

Layout & Manor of Barking

Bibliography & Further Reading

Timeline

626–655	Reign of Penda, pagan warrior-king of Mercia. Cynewise was his queen. Their daughters established a monastery in Peterborough and were venerated as saints. Tibba was the patron saint of falconers
c639	Birth of Aldhelm, the Bishop of Sherborne, a renowned scholar and the first Anglo-Saxon to write in Latin verse. His *'de laude de virginitatis'* is addressed to the nuns of Barking.
657	Hild of Whitby founds Streanæshealh Abbey (Whitby).
657-684	Cædmon, earliest known poet in English, monk at Streanæshealh.
664	Outbreak in Britain of the 'Yellow Plague', which lasts about 20–25 years.
666	Æthelburh and her brother Earconwald found Barking Abbey.
673	Queen Æthelthryth (Saint Audrey) founds Ely Abbey.
c673–735	Venerable Bede, monk at Monkwearmouth-Jarrow Abbey, the "father of English history".
695	Death of Æthelburh.
695–700	Hildelith, abbess at Barking.
709	Death of Aldhelm.
c725	Death of Hildelith.
731	Bede completes his *Historia ecclesiastica gentis Anglorum*.
789	The first recorded Viking raid in Britain (Isle of Portland).
793	Viking raid on Lindisfarne, the official start of the Viking Age in Britain.
842	London besieged by Vikings, and again in 851.
855–869	Reign of Edmund "the martyr" – King of East Anglia, killed by Ivar the Boneless and Ubba.
870/871	Barking Abbey burnt to the ground along with its nuns.
959–975	Edgar "the peaceful" – King of the English.
937–1000	Life of Wulfthryth, Abbess of Wilton, lived for a year as Edgar's concubine.
965–70	Wulfhild's first tenure as abbess of Barking.
978–1013	Æthelred the Unready, King of the English.
985/6	Death of Harald Bluetooth, King of Denmark & Norway and father of Sweyn Forkbeard.

990–997	Wulfhild's second tenure as abbess of Barking.
1000–30	Lifledis, abbess at Barking.
1002	Gunhilde, Sweyn Forkbeard's sister, slain during St Brice's Day Massacre.
1009	Thorkell the Tall, a prominent Jomsviking, leads a Viking army to Kent.
1012	Disgusted by his troops' treatment of Archbishop Alphege, Thorkell defects to the English under Æthelred.
1013-14	Forkbeard, the first Danish King of England.
1014	Wulfstan "Lupus Episcopus", Archbishop of York writes his *Sermo lupi ad Anglos* (Sermon of the wolf to the English).
1014–16	Æthelred "the Unready" regains the throne.
1016-35	Cnut the Great, son of Sweyn Forkbeard, is King of all England.
1042-66	Edward the Confessor, King of the English.
1045	Edith of Wessex, daughter of Godwin, marries Edward the Confessor.
1051	The Benedictine monk and noted goldsmith, Spearhafoc is elected as archbishop of London.
1052	Spearhafoc flees England when his consecration is refused.
1052–1100	Ælfgyva, abbess of Barking, she is 15 at her appointment.
1066	Harold Godwinson defeated by William at the Battle of Hastings, body identified by his first wife, Edyth the Gentle Swan ("Swan-neck").
1066	William "the Bastard" crowned King of England.
1091	Earliest reported tornado in England destroys parts of London.
1092	Roof of Old Sarum cathedral torn off in storm, days after its consecration.
1098	Birth of Saint Hildegard of Bingen, the German abbess and mystic. She was the author of significant visionary theological texts; books of science and medicine; hundreds of letters; and musical compositions for the liturgy.
1100–35	Reign of Henry I, King of England. Edith Forne was his concubine.
1120	Sinking of the White Ship and death of Henry I's heir, William Ætheling.
1135–53	The Anarchy, civil war in England precipitated by succession crisis.

1135–54	Stephen of Blois seizes the throne and becomes King of England.
1139	Henry I's daughter and chosen heir, Empress Mathilda, invades England.
1140–73	Adeliza, abbess at Barking; she founds the Ilford Hospital Chapel.
1141–48	Mathilda is given title "Lady of the English", her war with Stephen ends in stalemate, but her son Henry is declared Stephen's successor.
1144	Jews of Norwich falsely accused of the ritual murder of William of Norwich.
1154–89	Henry II, King of England; his wife and queen consort was Eleanor of Aquitaine, who spent 16 years of Henry's reign imprisoned by him.
1160–1215	Marie de France, one of the earliest recorded female authors in Europe, flourished.
1163–1200	Clémence of Barking, author of the *Life of St Catherine*, flourished.
1166–1216	John, King of England.
1170	Murder of Thomas Becket.
1173–75	Mary Becket, abbess of Barking, possible identity of Marie de France.
1179	Death of Hildegard of Bingen.
1189–90	Massacres of Jews at London and York.
1189–99	Richard I, King of England.
1196	Execution of William "Longbeard" Fitz Osbert, for inciting an uprising of the poor against the 'heaviness of rich men's hands'.
1200–15	Christiana de Valoniis, abbess of Barking.
1209	King John excommunicated by Pope Innocent III.
1215	Magna Carta.
1216	King John loses his crown in the Wash, dying shortly after of dysentery.
1216–72	Henry III, King of England; his wife was Eleanor of Provence; she died 1291.
1253	Henry III introduces his Statute of Jewry, imposing segregation on the Jews of Britain.
1255	Murder of Hugh of Lincoln, the most well-known of the pernicious blood libel accusations against the Jews of Britain.

1258–91	Maud de Leveland, abbess of Barking
1272–1307	Edward I, King of England, also known as "Longshanks" and "The Hammer of the Scots".
1276–1291	Alice de Merton, abbess of Barking.
1281	Edward I orders the extermination of all wolves in England.
1287	England struck by two devastating storms, one of which occurred on St Lucia's Day. One of the largest floods in recorded history.
1290	Edict of Expulsion, Edward I expels all Jews from England.
1310	Marguerite Porete burnt at the stake for heresy.
1313–14	Elizabeth de Burgh, wife of Robert the Bruce held captive at Barking Abbey.
1315–1317	Height of the Great Famine in Europe.
1318	Anne de Vere, abbess of Barking dies in office.
1318–29	Eleanor de Weston, abbess of Barking.
1341–52	Maud Montagu (senior) abbess of Barking, succeeded by her sister Isabel, and then later, her niece, also Maud.
1343–1416	Life of the anchoress and mystic, Julian of Norwich, author of *Revelations of Divine Love*.
1346	Battle of Crécy.
1348	Joan of England, daughter of Edward III and Philippa of Hainault dies in a small village near Bordeaux from the Black Death.
1348	The Black Death arrives in Britain.
1348–1400	Life of Alice Perrers, mistress of Edward III in his later years, and inspiration for Chaucer's Wife of Bath.
1358–77	Katherine de Sutton, abbess of Barking.
1361	The Pestilence of Boys, resurgence of the plague affecting boys in particular.
1364–1430	Life of Christine de Pizan, considered one of the earliest feminist writers, author of *The Book of the City of Ladies*.
1373–1438	Life of Margery Kempe, mystic and author of the first autobiography in English, *The Book of Margery Kempe*.
1377–93	Maud Montagu (niece of Maud Montagu senior) abbess of Barking.
1377–99	Richard II King of England, he was 10 when he succeeded to the throne.
1380	The mystic and activist, Catherine of Siena dies in Rome.
1381	Peasants' Revolt in England.

1382	Earthquake Synod at Blackfriars, convened to discuss Lollards and the teachings of John Wycliffe. Named for the Dover Straits earthquake that was felt in London at the time.
1394	Death of Anne of Bohemia, Queen Consort of Richard II, from the plague.
1400–52	Life of Eleanor Cobham, wife of Humphrey Duke of Gloucester.
1412–31	Life of Joan of Arc, burnt at the stake for the heresy of cross-dressing.
1415	Wycliffe posthumously declared a heretic, his writings banned.
1428	Wycliffe's body exhumed, burned and thrown into the river Swift.
1433–73	Katherine de la Pole, longest-standing abbess of Barking, was in her early 20s when she was appointed.
1441	Margery Jourdemayne, "The Witch of Ey" burnt at the stake for treasonable necromancy.
1445	Henry VI, King of England marries Margaret of Anjou.
1445–1527	Elizabeth "Jane" Shore, mistress of Edward IV; accused of conspiracy by Edward's successor Richard III.
1450	Mock-trial and subsequent beheading of William de la Pole at sea near Dover.
1450	Jack Cade's Rebellion.
1455–87	The Wars of the Roses.
1461	Battle of Towton, reputedly the bloodiest ever battle on English soil.
1470	Jacquetta of Luxembourg, cleared of witchcraft by the council of Edward IV. Tried a second time in 1484, but again cleared.
1485-1536	Life of Katherine of Aragon, first wife of King Henry VIII (1509–33).
1484	Pope Innocent VIII issues the *Summis desiderantes affectibus,* a papal bull regarding witchcraft that sanctioned the work of the Inquisition.
1486	Publication of the *Malleus Maleficarum,* the Hammer of Witches.
1507–36	Life of Anne Boleyn , second wife (1533-36) of King Henry VIII.
1508–37	Life of Jane Seymour, third wife (1536-37) of King Henry VIII.

1508–39	Thomasina Jenney, prioress at Barking.
1516	Birth of Mary I.
1523	*The education of a Christian woman*, Juan Luis Vives, written for Mary I.
1526	*A devout treatise upon the Pater Noster*, Margaret Roper (née More)'s translation of Erasmus.
1527–39	Dorothy Barley, final abbess of Barking.
1533	Birth of Elizabeth I.
1535	Execution for treason of Thomas More, the Renaissance humanist and author of *Utopia*.
1536–41	Dissolution of the Monasteries, including all monasteries, priories, convents and friaries in England, Wales and Ireland.
1536–37	Pilgrimage of Grace, popular uprising in the north of England.
1539	The Surrender of Barking Abbey under Dorothy Barley.

Characters

<u>Invented or surmised</u> –
The wives and washerwomen of Barking; Merle (the wishing wif); Thora (chief washerwoman); the woodsman's wife and Sisters Eleanor, Dulcie, Sabine, Olive, Cecilia and Julian.

<u>Historical</u> –
All other characters are named in the histories of Barking Abbey or are relations thereof; anyone appearing in the hics are likewise historical. Dates of tenure as abbess are sometimes approximate. The book is not an exhaustive account of the abbesses of Barking, there were many others whose lives are lost to history.

<u>Adeliza</u> – Abbess, 1140–73. Adeliza founded a hospice-chapel at Ilford, just up the Roding from Barking. Later enlarged by Mary Becket, it is still there today.
<u>Ælfgyva</u> – Abbess, 1052–1100. Ælfgyva was made abbess unexpectedly at the age of 15, she would later rebuild significant sections of the abbey and translate the bones of Æthelburh, Hildelith and Wulfhild in order to enlarge the church. She commissioned Goscelin of St Bertin's *Lives of the Abbesses at Barking*. Buried in the arch against the high altar.
<u>Æthelburh</u> – Abbess, 666–95. Æthelburh was the founder of Barking Abbey alongside her brother Earconwald, who also founded Chertsey. He later became Bishop of London and died at Barking. Æthelburh was sainted and miracles are associated with her.
<u>Dorothy Barley</u> – Abbess 1527–39. Sister of Henry Barley, who was a member of parliament. Henry left Dorothy a doublet and 40 shillings in his will. In the end she received a generous pension, the second largest awarded to the head of a nunnery. She died in 1557.
<u>Mary Becket</u> – Abbess, 1173–75. Mary was made abbess of Barking by Henry II as recompense for the murder of her brother, Thomas Becket. Some theories suggest she was the true identity of the poet Marie de France. I embrace that possibility here. Buried in the arch before the altar of Our Lady and St Paul, in the aisle.
<u>The Cellaress</u> – we do not have a name for the nun who wrote the *Charthe longynge to the Office of Celeresse of the Monasterye of Barkinge*, but my poem is an adaptation of this charter, which she wrote for the benefit of her successors.

Clémence – Poet & nun, flourished in the latter third of the 12th century. An Anglo-Norman poet-translator at Barking, she wrote a *Life* of the martyred saint, Catherine of Alexandria.

Hildelith – Abbess, 695–700, was initially Æthelburh's teacher, she lived to a grand old age, dying c725. Her section should span two centuries, but as her tenure as abbess ended by 700, I have kept her in the 7th century. Bede's account of Barking was written in the early 700s.

Thomasina Jenney – Prioress 1508–39.

Maud de Leveland – Abbess 1258–75, resigned her office. Buried near the altar of our Lady of Salvation.

Lifledis – Abbess, 1000–30, not much is known about her but she was responsible for the translation of Wulfhild's bones to be near those of Æthelburh and Hildelith, in the choir of the original church at Barking.

Alice de Merton – Abbess 1276–91, died in office. Buried in an arch against the cemetery.

Maud Montagu, senior – Abbess 1341–52, died in office at height of the Black Death. During the latter half of the 14th century, three Montagus held the title of Abbess at Barking, Maud senior, her sister Isabel, and their niece Maud (below). Buried in the quire.

Maud Montagu, younger – Abbess 1377–93, niece of Maud Montagu senior (above) and daughter of Edward Montagu and Alice of Norfolk, the granddaughter of Edward I. Alice was murdered by her husband and his retainers when Maud was a child. Maud was buried in an arch before the high altar, against the door of the vestry.

Katherine de la Pole – Abbess for forty years 1433–73, died in office. She was the sister of William "Jackanapes" de la Pole, whose wife was Geoffrey Chaucer's granddaughter, Alice. Both Alice and Katherine had considerable libraries.

Katherine de Sutton – Abbess 1358–77, died in office. Katherine commissioned a new set of Easter plays that influenced the development of theatrical works in England, France and Germany. Buried in an arch in the Chapel of our Lady.

Tortgyth – Novice mistress at the time of both Æthelburh and Hildelith, she had a vision concerning Æthelburh's death that helped to cement the reputation of the abbey.

The Unnamed – Around 870/871 the abbey was attacked by Vikings and razed to the ground, with all the nuns burnt to death. We have no names for these women. The abbey was not restored until a century later.

Christiana de Valoniis – Abbess, 1200–15, buried in the middle of the chapter, under a marble stone.

Anne de Vere – Abbess, died in office, probably from hunger, at the height of the Great Famine, in 1318. Buried before the shrine of St. Hildelith.

Eleanor de Weston – Abbess 1318–29, sought permission from Edward II to fell 300 forest oaks at a time when the abbey had fallen into disrepair.

Wulfhild – Abbess, 965–70 and again 990–97. Wulfhild was the re-founder of Barking Abbey, a century after its having been razed by the Danes. The abbey was given to her by Edgar the Peaceful. She was later removed from her position and sent to Horton Abbey by Edgar's queen, Ælfthryth, who later restored her as abbess at Barking. Wulfhild was sainted, miracles are associated with her.

Wulfruna – Sacristan, early to mid-11th century, also known as Judith. She was very close to Abbess Wulfhild, who appeared to her in a vision.

Notes

A rose of shimmering –
Hic: Æthelburh's brother Earconwald was Bishop of London from 675–93.

Poem: although its history is obscure, it is thought that Berecingchirche, or All Hallows-by-the-Tower, was founded by Barking Abbey during Æthelburh's tenure. It is perhaps the oldest church in the City of London. *Still unsettled graves* – Barking was initially a double monastery with separate communities of both nuns and monks. Double monasteries were forbidden after 787. In Bede's account of Æthelburh's miracle, the graves belonged to monks who had recently died of the 'yellow plague', which began in England in 664 and lasted 20–25 years. The onset of the plague coincided with a solar eclipse and was likely an outbreak of the first plague pandemic in Europe.

Shucked and cast away –
Poem: it is thought that Æthelburh and her brother were from the minor Anglo-Saxon kingdom of Lindsey, present-day Lincolnshire. The royal house of Lindsey liked to trace its ancestors back to the Anglo-Saxon god, Woden. For the Latin, see Book of Job 13:28 and 30:17.

Seigneur en jupe –
Poem: it is not certain where Hildelith came from, but the abbey at Chelles is a good contender. *Tout mes sources fraîches en Toi* is an adaptation of a line from Psalm 87,7.

Letters –
Poems: influenced by passages in Aldhelm's riddle poems and his *De Laude Virginitatis*, also Bede's *Historia ecclesiastica gentis Anglorum*. The hymn, *O Gloriosa Domina* is a plainsong melody in the Ionian mode.

The bloody welkin –
Hic: in Abbo of Fleury's account of Edmund the Martyr's murder, Edmund's severed head calls out to be found *hic, hic, hic* ("here, here, here") where it is found protected by a wolf. Barking was razed in the 9th century and remained disused for a century after. The sisters, for whom we have no names, were all burned to death.

Poem: Scholastica was the twin sister of Saint Benedict and foundress of the Benedictine nuns. She is the patron saint of convulsive children and rain. Knowing she was about to die she asked her brother to stay with her. When he refused to listen, she prayed and God sent a storm to keep him with her. The final passage is an anachronistic riff on Burchard of Worms' *De paenitentia*. 'Mōdraniht', or Night of the Mothers, was a winter solstice festival. The Anglo-Saxon words are all descriptors used of women: hags, witches, maidens, sibyls, wise women etc. Also, secrets and witchcraft.

Bright, as with comets falling –
Hic: Edgar the Peaceful had a bit of a thing for nuns. He abducted Wulfthryth, a novice and later abbess at Wilton. Their daughter was the flamboyant saint, Edith of Wilton, whom Goscelin (in his Life of Edith) says was a 'remote' abbess of Barking. Edgar also tried to abduct Wulfhild, when she too was a novice at Wilton. He made amends for this by rebuilding Barking Abbey for her. His wife Ælfthryth later deposed Wulfhild but subsequently restored her, having been spooked by a dream.

Poem: See Bede and Aldhelm for early-medieval glass windows.

With breath and hem –
Hic: there are two legends associated with Wulfhild's death. Firstly, when her body was brought home to Barking the coffin became unbearably heavy due to a sinner's hand touching it. Secondly, at the translation of her bones thirty years later, the hand of a woman whom Wulfhild had criticised in life for hoarding gold, had a similar effect (see *A bundle of myrrh*).

Poem: the duties of a sacristan included care of ceremonial objects. Generally speaking women were not allowed to serve in the chancel, but this was permitted in a convent. See *The Nun Who Loved the World* for the 13th-century story of Beatrice, a sacristan. Candlemas is the Feast of the Purification of Mary and is the point in the church calendar when candles for the year are blessed. For quotes, see Exodus 28:34; 38:8; 39:25; Psalm 45:1. The full text of *Revertere, revertere, quene of blisse and beaute* can be found in Richard Greene's *A Selection of English Carols*.

Remedies –
Hic: St Brice's Day Massacre – in 1002 Æthelred the Unready ordered the killing of all Danes in England, arguably precipitating events that would lead to Cnut becoming king in 1016.

Poem: an adaptation of Anglo-Saxon pregnancy charms found in the *Lacnunga* and known collectively as 'For Delayed Birth'. The charms are unique in that they were intended to be recited specifically by women. The poem focuses solely on the charm to rectify an inability to conceive. '*Mihtig wif*' – 'powerful woman'.

Boundary –
Hic: see *Sermo Lupi ad Anglos* (Sermon of the Wolf to the English), by Wulfstan, Archbishop of York; he served under both Æthelred and Cnut, and wrote the laws issued by the later in 1021.

Poem: see Acts 20:29 and Song of Solomon 3:6. '*Peace to the cherishers of peace*' – Vera Morton's translation of a line from Goscelin de St Bertin's *Lives of the Abbesses at Barking* (the shaky Latin is mine).

In medio choro –
Hic: The Isle of Thorney (Westminster) is one suggested location for Cnut's famous demonstration of our helplessness before an incoming tide. For Osbern's wonderful account of the translation of Alphege's remains from St Paul's to Canterbury, see Clerk of Oxford. Osbern alleges Alphege's uncorrupted body was conveyed in a gold-prowed longboat steered singlehandedly by Cnut across the Thames, and then on by cart. London was not happy to lose the saint's remains.

Poem: the translation of holy relics, or a saint's body, to a location of higher status would involve great ceremony and the presence of the community. Abbess Lifledis moved Wulhid's remains to be nearer those of Æthelburh and Hildelith. The bones of all three would be moved again about fifty years later by Abbess Ælfgyva.

A bundle of myrrh –
Poem: see 'Breath and hem' note above re legends of Wulfhild; also Song of Solomon 1:13, 4:11, 4:12, 5:5, 7:8.

Girl abbess –
Hic & Poem: Ælfgyva commissioned Goscelin of St Bertin's *Lives of the Abbesses at Barking*; Goscelin was a close friend and advisor of Eve of Wilton, who had a vision concerning him. Ælfgyva's dream is modelled on this. Intense spiritual relationships between monks and nuns were a

trope of the period, but I have invented the relationship between Ælfgyva and the renegade bishop Spearhafoc. This invention was partly inspired by the *Et Ælfgyva* panel in the Bayeux tapestry, in which a metal worker, who appears to be a cleric, can be seen embroidered in the margin below Ælfgyva. Spearhafoc ("sparrowhawk") was a noted goldsmith and was elected to the Archbishopric of London in 1051 but was never consecrated. He was expelled from London and fled the country with several bags of treasure, including jewels and gold entrusted to him by Edward the Confessor. Edward's wife, Edith of Wessex, gave Spearhafoc a ring, which was involved in a miracle connected with him. Edward dispatched Edith to a nunnery most likely because she was childless. This was at the time of her father, Godwin, Earl of Wessex's rebellion; the ships in the Thames are his. The 'babes trampled' is a reference to the altercation between Eustace, Count of Boulogne, and with the citizens of Dover, which precipitated Godwin's fall from grace. Queen Dido was the founder of Carthage and a popular point of comparison for an abbess. The nuns of Barking would have been aware of Virgil's *Aeneid* in which Dido appears. This section, and the two following, nod to scenes in Books 1 and 4 of the *Aeneid.* See also Job 39:26.

Cusp and corbel –
Hic & Poem: following his coronation at Westminster Abbey, William the Conqueror stayed at Barking Abbey for three months where he received the surrender of many of the great earls of England. He and his wife Matilda of Flanders were keen builders of abbeys and castles. Edyth Swanneck was the first wife of Harold, whose mutilated body she was reputed to have identified on the battlefield. The various quotes: Song of Songs 2:5; Job 38:4; Isaiah 54: 1 & 2; Psalms 31:8.

Settle down muddy beds –
Hic: Edith Forne was the concubine of Henry I. Her dream of magpies is painted beside her tomb. Beatrix was the mother of the anchoress and visionary, Christina of Markyate; she was pregnant with Christina at the time of the dove in the sleeve, which she interpreted as signifying Christina's future holiness. I have merged two storms into one: there was an incredibly destructive tornado in London, October 1091, with winds estimated at 240 miles per hour; also in 1092, five days after its consecration, the roof of Old Sarum Cathedral was torn off in a storm. Saint Benedict's sister Scholastica was the patron saint of convulsive children and was invoked against storms.

Poem: urine, moonlight and frost were all considered useful bleaching agents. Winterfylleð, was the first full moon of winter, it was also the time of the Great Wash. The veil is inspired by the one given to Dido by Aeneas and, previously, to Helen of Troy by her mother Leda. See Proverbs, 30:4 and Jeremiah 14:6 for some of the storm language.

Red-capped –
Hic: the sinking of the White Ship prompted a succession crisis in England that resulted in the period of British history known as The Anarchy. Henry I nominated his daughter Matilda as heir, but the Anglo-Norman barons couldn't stomach the idea of a female ruler. Despite being married, Matilda styled herself as an autonomous woman, a 'feme sole' – see medieval laws of Coverture for concepts of feme sole/feme covert. The infirmary at Ilford was established on assart land granted by King Stephen and is still standing today; Stephen's queen (another Matilda) established St Katharine's by the Tower, a similar hospice at about the same time.

Poem: a 'cure' for leprosy is found in Hildegard of Bingen's *Physica (Causae et Curae)*, in which she says to 'make a bath and mix in as much menstrual blood as you can get'. Hildegard talks a lot about viridity/floridity in context with this 'cure'. There is a cleansing ritual for leprosy in Leviticus involving cedar, scarlet, hyssop and the blood of a bird. See also John, 6:53 and Leviticus 17:11 – *for the life of the flesh is in the blood.*

Lark-tongued –
Hic: Abbess Tengswych of Andernach wrote to Hildegard of Bingen regarding the latter's somewhat 'exuberant' worship. The Crusades were a period of punitive taxation, for which the Jewish communities in Britain were scapegoated. This was the period in which the pernicious 'blood libel' myths began to circulate. It is unclear which nun at Barking translated Ælred's *Life of Edward the Confessor* as the text is anonymous; this was common at the time, but both Clémence (an Anglo-Norman poet-translator at Barking), and her contemporary the 12th-century poet Marie-de France, emphatically name themselves in their own work. Clémence penned a life of the 4th-century saint Catherine of Alexandria, whose eloquence (dismissed by Emperor Maxentius as 'silly girl ravings' (*frivola puelle deliramenta*)) was a popular source of inspiration. Clémence's book is now regarded as a proto-feminist text. Both she and Marie de France were passionate about translation into the vernacular to make texts more widely available.

Poem: Catherine of Alexandria was martyred at 18. Scourged then imprisoned without food, it was said that she had been fed by a dove and her wounds healed by angels. When her cell was opened there was a bright light and perfume, and she emerged radiant. Sentenced to the 'breaking wheel', it burst into pieces at her touch, killing 4,000 pagan spectators. She was then beheaded, and milk was said to flow from her neck. In 800 CE, her body was allegedly found on Mount Sinai, exuding a healing balm. A shrine was established at Westminster around a phial of this balm brought back to England by Edward the Confessor.

Men were not so clever then, nor so envious as they are now –
Hic: the remarkable Eleanor of Aquitaine was imprisoned for sixteen years by her husband Henry II for supporting their younger son Henry's revolt against him; their son Richard (the Lion Heart) later succeeded him. Richard released Eleanor from prison, and she acted as regent in his absence. Eleanor was a patron of writers, led armies and was one of the wealthiest and most powerful women in the Middle Ages. She refused to take the veil and outlived sons, mistresses, bishops, kings. She would undoubtedly have known the poet, Marie de France. William Fitz Osbert was an advocate of the poor, for which he was hanged, drawn and quartered. Objects connected with him were venerated, including the soil beneath his gibbet.

Poem: Mary was the sister of Thomas Becket; she was made abbess of Barking as recompense for the murder of her brother by the king. Some theories point to her being the identity of Marie de France, a possibility I embrace here. The title is taken from McBain's translation of Clémence's *Vie de Sainte Catherine*. 'Brought to a river, reeking and deep' is from *L'Espurgatoire Seint Patriz*, and 'The one who forgets oneself is foolish. Here I write my name Marie…' is from the Epilogue to the *Vie Seinte Audree*, both of which are commonly attributed to Marie de France. For the life of St Audrey, see the letter from Osbert of Clare to Adeliza, Abbess of Barking. Guernes de Pont-Sainte-Maxence was a 12th-century scribe, who wrote a contemporary account of Thomas Becket's murder. Guernes lost his first version of this text, so took the opportunity to visit Barking to interview Mary about her brother's life before re-writing. The quotes are from his letter thanking her for her hospitality. Novices at Barking Abbey were, uniquely, referred to as *scholares*.

Massacre of the innocents –
Hic: a grisly story, Maud de Braose (*aka* Moll Wallbee), initially a favourite of King John, was later starved to death by him in Corfe Castle along with her son. There are several Welsh legends about her. In 1216 King John lost the crown jewels whilst crossing a tidal estuary near the Wash in a rushed bid to stop an invasion from the north. The apocryphal 'surfeit of peaches' would not have sat well with a man suffering from dysentery.

Poem: Childermas, or the Feast of the Holy Innocents was held on 28th December to mark Herod's execution of all boys two years and under in the vicinity of Bethlehem; these boys were regarded as the first Christian martyrs. At Barking and elsewhere a *puerilia solemnia* was celebrated, but it was also the season of misrule when a child abbot or abbess was elected. The Fool's Abbess had the run of the abbey and would go out raising donations. These activities were increasingly frowned upon by the church fathers, especially when children took part in the rituals of the *puerilia solemnia* itself.

Menagerie –
Hic: the boy-king is Henry III; his queen, Eleanor of Provence was loathed by Londoners, who once attacked her barge with loose paving stones and vegetables. Renowned for her cleverness, beauty, poetry and love of fashion, she is the only English queen without a marked grave. Henry spent a fortune on shrines, festivals, castles and overseas campaigns. During his early years the Jewish community flourished, but he later crippled them financially. This ultimately fuelled anti-Jewish sentiment because of their need to recover debts. Henry introduced The Statute of Jewry, which amongst other restrictions decreed all Jews should wear a yellow badge on their chest. The places mentioned were scenes of atrocities, though this is not an exhaustive list.

Poem: Henry established a zoo at the Tower of London, including a large elephant house that would later be used to imprison members of the Jewish community. It was a period of conspicuous gift giving by heads of state and Henry received wild animals from King Haakon of Norway, the King of France, and the Holy Roman Emperor. For final quote, see Job 12:10.

Enclosure –
Hic: a period of climate change leading to the beginning of the Little Ice Age in Europe. In 1290 Edward Longshanks introduced the Edict of

Expulsion, by which all Jews were ordered to leave England no later than All Saints Day; see Holinshed's *Chronicles* for their treatment at the Isle of Sheppey.

Poem: a found poem, made largely out of translations and paraphrases of injunctions found in Eileen Power's *Medieval English Nunneries*. Her book references the *Epistles* of John Peckham (Archbishop of Canterbury) and the *Constitutions* of Cardinal Legate, Ottobon de Fieschi, who for a while lived at the Tower of London and who later became Pope Adrian V.

The great famine –
Hic: The *King and Queen of the May* are Robert the Bruce and his wife, Elizabeth de Burgh. Elizabeth was confined at Barking Abbey between 1313–14. Edward Longshanks was known as the Hammer of the Scots.

Poem: The Great Famine occurred between 1315–17 and coincided with the end of the Medieval Warm Period. Appalling weather conditions meant nothing could grow. See Revelations, 6:17, "For the great day of his wrath is come; and who shall be able to stand?"

Morsel –
Hic: the beguine and mystic Marguerite Porete was burnt at the stake for heresy and for her refusal to withdraw her book *The Mirror of Simple Souls*, which detailed the stages of annihilation a soul must go through, en route to oneness with God through love. Beguines were religious women committed to emulating Christ through voluntary poverty and care of the sick. They took no formal vows, but lived in small communities of like-minded women.

Poem: in addition to Porete, the nothingness is also informed by one of Jacopone da Todi's *Lauds*.

The great pestilence –
Hic: Joan of England was the daughter of Edward III and Philippa of Hainault. When Joan left for Europe to marry, the Black Death (or Great Pestilence as it was then known) had not yet taken hold in England, she died of the plague within weeks of reaching Boulogne and was thus among the first English people to die of it. She was fourteen.

Poem: once the Black Death took hold in England it is thought between 40-60% of the population died, with boys and men being particularly affected. Coming so soon after the Great Famine, the plague would plunge Europe into crisis as well as disenchantment with both church and state. The consequent shortage of labour resulted in a rise in wages. Landowners resisted this rise and imposed restrictions on movement. Stocks were built in every town to punish idlers.

The harrowing of hell –
Hic: Catherine of Siena (1347–80), Italian mystic and writer. Rare for women in the church at that time, Catherine was granted significant autonomy by the Pope, whom she called Babbo or 'Daddy'. There was a miracle associated with her head, which was posthumously severed; she died from extreme fasting. Julian of Norwich, was an English anchoress, who, after suffering a near death experience in 1373, wrote *Revelations of Divine Love*, an account of her visions of the Passion of Christ. Alice Perrers was the daughter of a thatcher, and mistress to King Edward III, who endowed her with several estates. She had quite a head for business and became the wealthiest woman in the country. Ambitious and independent, she refused to play ball with church and state, and is believed to be the model for Chaucer's Wife of Bath and Langland's Lady Mede. When the Abbot of St Albans sued her over a land dispute, she appeared in court, which scandalised people. After Edward died, an ordinance was drawn up that forbade women, and in particular Alice, from using their influence in a court of law. Walsingham's contemporary account of her was especially misogynistic. In his words, *she far overstepped the bounds of feminine conduct: forgetful of her sex and her weakness.*

Poem: Katherine de Sutton commissioned a new set of Easter plays that influenced the development of theatrical works in England, France and Germany. At a time of concern about acedia, or spiritual sluggishness, Katherine was keen to engage her apathetic congregation by increasing the theatrical element of the plays. She also allowed women to play significant characters in these liturgical dramas, which was an innovation. The quotes are all taken from the Easter plays at Barking, with some of the language of the '*N-town Plays*'. For 'ydelnesse' see Chaucer's Second Nun's Tale. The embroidered hellmouth is influenced by the descent into Hades in Aeneid VI. There is debate as to whether it should be 'ad infernos' or 'ad *inferos*', the former would suggest the flames of hell, the later simply 'below'. Either way, to Hell! *Corrodies* were a form of pension: a lifetime allowance of food, shelter etc. that could be demanded of a monastery by the king, for someone of his choosing. Katherine's letter is a fiction.

The worth of a penny –
1st hic: the boy-king is Richard II, who was only ten when he came to the throne of England and fourteen at the time of the Peasants' Revolt, the suppression of which he played a significant role in. His wife Anne of Bohemia died of the plague at 28.

1st poem: although a failure, the Peasants' Revolt or Great Rising was the beginning of the English people's fight for freedom from the feudal system. The uprising was provoked by years of brutal taxation, privation and disease, with the last trigger being the poll taxes of 1377, 79 and 81. The taxes were applied to anyone with pubic hair and were particularly hard on widowed mothers. Many women were active in the uprising. Ironically, given he betrayed them, the rebel slogan was, *With King Richard and the true commons.* The king's uncle was John of Gaunt, the close friend and brother-in-law of Geoffrey Chaucer. Initially, Gaunt was a supporter of the religious reformer, John Wycliffe.

2nd hic: the 'poor fathers' were followers of Wycliffe, otherwise known as Lollards. Wycliffe was a theologian and biblical translator, he questioned the wealth and pomp of the church, and preached reform. The 'priest of England's village green' is the roving preacher John Ball who espoused similar views. People were forbidden to hear him preach. The synod at Blackfriars was called to discuss the suppression of Wycliffe's teachings and was interrupted by an earthquake. Wycliffe was posthumously excommunicated for heresy and his books outlawed and burned. Several of Wycliffe books are known to have been at Barking. Joan Hancock and Agnes Jenkin were imprisoned for speaking out; they were freed by protestors during the Peasants' Revolt. Catherine of Siena is buried above a temple of Isis in Rome.

2nd poem: kiddles were banned because they allowed a monopoly over the fish entering the mouth of a river. In 1454 London surveyors implementing Magna Carta rules regarding kiddles were attacked by armed groups from Woolwich, Erith and Barking and chased off with the cry of "Hence, traitors of London!"

3rd hic: 'away with the learning of clerks, away with it!' was a slogan of the rebels in Cambridge during the Peasants' Revolt, words largely attributed to Margery Starre. The rebels burnt the library and archives of the university, destroying charters and records of debt. As described by Dan Jones, Margery embodied a 'spirit of jubilant vandalism'. Johanna Ferrour led the attack on John of Gaunt's lavish palace on Fleet Street, which was dismantled then torched. Although motivated by principle, the rebellion led by Wat Tyler and John Ball had its dark side, one that was felt with horrible inevitability by outsiders and immigrants, in particular the Flemish weavers of London.

3rd poem: Edward Montagu was the father of Maud Montagu, the younger. He was an all-round shit. *Their full weight and weapons* is taken from the report of the attack on his wife Alice of Norfolk.

<u>Mustard, and salt biscuits</u> –
Hic: 'Roaring Margery' is the English Christian mystic, Margery Kempe, whose *Book* is considered the first autobiography in English. She travelled widely.

Poem: an adaptation of the undated account written by an unnamed cellaress. Her *Charthe longynge to the Office of the Celeresse of the Monasterye of Barkinge* was written for the guidance of her successors. I have referred to the William Dugdale translation, and to those phrases in the Rule of St Benedict that are pertinent to her role. I have re-imagined these materials into four shopping / to-do lists as might be scribbled on scraps of paper. A *pottle* of Tyre (a decent drop of Lebanese medieval plonk) was rather more than a *bottle* thereof, more like half a gallon.

<u>Hic liber constat</u> –
Hic: Christine de Pizan wrote *Le livre de la Cité des Dames*, as well as *Le Ditie de Jehanne d'Arc*, a celebration of Joan of Arc written before Joan's eventual death at the stake for heresy.

Poem: a fusion of some of the books known to have been in the library of Katherine de la Pole; descriptions of book bindings in the library of her sister-in-law, Alice Chaucer; plus, one or two speculative tomes. We know of Katherine's library from the will of William Pownsett, chief steward at Barking; the phrase *'certayne bookes…'* comes from his will. The library at Barking no doubt also contained some of the books belonging to Sibyl de Felton, who was both abbess at Barking (1393–1419) and a notable collector.

Dolls of lead –

1st hic: Eleanor Cobham was married to Humphrey, Duke of Gloucester, who was next in line to the throne. They were a flamboyant pair. Eleanor consulted Margery Jourdemayne, 'the Witch of Ey' for a charm to conceive a child but was later tried along with others for treasonable necromancy against the King. She was found guilty and sentenced to public atonement and life imprisonment. Eleanor's fellow-accused were all killed, with Margery being burnt at the stake. Katherine de la Pole's brother was involved in the later arrest of Humphrey. *Heart and belly of a man* – there were descriptions at the time of the strength and courage of Margaret of Anjou (wife of Henry VI, in whose stead she ruled for 18 month, while he was unwell). Edward Hall described her as "of stomach and courage, more like to a man". Her involvement on the Lancastrian side of what would later be called The Wars of the Roses is well documented, as is her defeat at the Battle of Towton, the bloodiest ever battle on British soil. Jacquetta of Luxembourg was mother of Elizabeth Woodville, wife of Edward IV. She was House of Lancaster then later House of York. She was tried for witchcraft but found not guilty.

1st poem: Humphrey, Duke of Gloucester paid for the construction of the Bodleian and supplied it with hundreds of books. The Bodleian's oldest reading room is named after him.

2nd hic: Richard Wyche, vicar of Deptford and a Lollard, was burnt at the stake. The then vicar of All Hallows, Thomas Virby, confessed in prison to having mixed spices in with Wyche's ashes to deceive the poor (sweet smelling remains being deemed evidence of sanctity). Katherine de la Pole's brother William "Jackanapes" was deeply unpopular. He was viewed as a symbol of the corruption surrounding the King, and of the oppression of the regime. He was banished but was later murdered en route to France. When his body was found on the beach at Dover, the people of Kent were concerned about retaliation. Jake Cade led a crowd of thousands to London, where despite intentions they turned to looting and battles on London Bridge.

Tender mothers –

Hic: Elizabeth Shore (known more commonly now as 'Jane' due to a 17th-century invention), was a mistress of Edward IV. Thomas More described her in later life as 'intelligent, literate, merry and playful' and said that the attractiveness which drew many to her, resided in her personality. She was very well educated for the daughter of a draper and was accused of conspiracy by Richard III. The Hammer of Witches or *Malleus Maleficarum* is a famous treatise on witchcraft that contributed to the sinister and vicious persecution of women in the early modern period; likewise, Pope Innocent VIII's bull regarding the same.

Poem: an Anglicised adaptation of 13th-century hymns to the Virgin (*De la tres douce Marie; Serena virginum; o maria o felix puerpera;* and, *O maria virginei*) beautiful renditions of which can be heard on Anonymous 4's *la bele marie* (a collection of songs drawn from Latin liturgy or the vernacular songs of the trouvères).

"Syng ye wysely and intentyuely" – Chapter 19, the Rule of St Benedict.

<u>If not for her sex, she could have defied</u> –
Hic: *If not for her sex, she could have defied all the heroes of History* – Thomas Cromwell's description of Henry VIII's first wife Katherine of Aragon. In response to an invasion by the Scots while Henry was in France on a military campaign, Katherine led the army north in full armour while heavily pregnant. When she first came to England, Katherine had a retinue of African attendants; these were the first documented Africans in London. One attendant, depicted in tournament rolls of the time, was John Blanke the trumpeter. Another was Catalina, Katherine's mistress of the bedchamber. Catalina (unlikely to have been her real name) left Spain a slave but returned there a freewoman. In later years she was tracked down to testify whether or not Katherine had been a virgin at the time of her marriage to Henry. 'The White Falcon' was written by Nicholas Udall for the lavish coronation of Henry's second wife Anne Boleyn. Anne was crowned with St Edward's crown, which was unprecedented for a queen consort. It has been suggested this was because she was visibly pregnant with what they hoped was a boy.

Poem: inspired by the list of tapestries in the inventory of St Mary's Nunnery at Langley from 1485.

<u>Unceasing choir</u> –
Hic: 'The Education of a Christian Woman' by Juan Luis Vives was commissioned by Katherine of Aragon for her daughter, Mary. The book was far from progressive, but was quite radical in that it insisted women

of all classes and abilities should have the right to an education, something that found favour with Erasmus and Thomas More, who believed in the education of women. More's daughter Margaret was the first ordinary woman to publish a translation. The Pilgrimage of Grace was a mass protest in Northern England against the dissolution of the monasteries (among other issues); it attracted many women to its cause. With no title or family to protect her, Margaret Cheyne was accused of 'enticing' her husband to 'raise the commons'. She was tortured and burned at the stake as a reminder to women not to promote rebellion, and for husbands not to listen to their wives.

Poem: the daughters are of course Mary I and Elizabeth I, both of whom were hearty babies. Mary's health issues did not begin until she reached puberty. William Petre was Henry VIII's Secretary of State and receiver of the surrender of Barking Abbey; he was a close friend of William Pownsett, the chief steward there. Petre did very well out of the dissolving of the abbey estate. In the end, he negotiated pensions for all the nuns of Barking, a luxury not afforded to the thousands of nuns across the country made homeless by the dissolution. Although Dorothy was not noble, she did come from a very comfortable family. Miraculous wimples etc. were used to gull the superstitious out of their money and were allegedly found at other monasteries.

Dissolution | the scattering of the beads –
Poem: list of nuns granted pensions at the surrender of Barking Abbey, 26th November 1539.

Epilogue –
Poem: Oak apples or galls, are formed by wasp larvae on the leaves of oak trees; they were the chief source of writing ink for the medieval, western world.

LAYOUT OF BARKING ABBEY

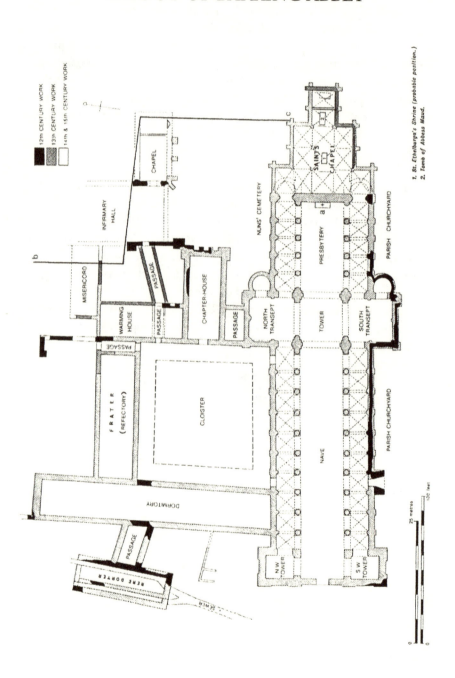

Legend:
- 12th CENTURY WORK
- 13th CENTURY WORK
- 14th & 15th CENTURY WORK

1. St. Ethelburga's Shrine (probable position.)
2. Tomb of Abbess Maud.

THE ANCIENT MANOR OF BARKING

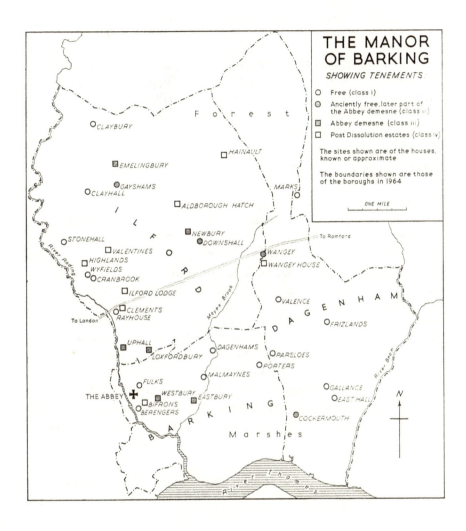

THE MANOR OF BARKING

SHOWING TENEMENTS

○ Free (class i)

◉ Anciently free, later part of the Abbey demesne (class ii)

▣ Abbey demesne (class iii)

☐ Post Dissolution estates (class iv)

The sites shown are of the houses, known or approximate

The boundaries shown are those of the boroughs in 1964

ONE MILE

Forest

○ CLAYBURY

☐ HAINAULT

▣ EMELINGBURY

◉ GAYSHAMS
○ CLAYHALL

MARKS

☐ ALDBOROUGH HATCH

I L F O R D

▣ NEWBURY
◉ DOWNSHALL

To Romford

○ STONEHALL

☐ VALENTINES

☐ HIGHLANDS
WYFIELDS
○ CRANBROOK

◉ WANGEY
☐ WANGEY HOUSE

☐ ILFORD LODGE

○ VALENCE

D A G E N H A M

☐ CLEMENTS
RAYHOUSE

To London

▣ UPHALL

☐ LOXFORDBURY

○ DAGENHAMS

☐ PARSLOES

☐ PORTERS

◉ FRIZLANDS

○ FULKS

○ MALMAYNES

○ GALLANCE

○ EAST HALL

THE ABBEY ✛

WESTBURY ▣ EASTBURY
☐ BIFRONS
○ BERENGERS

B A R K I N G

◉ COCKERMOUTH

N

Marshes

River Roding

Mayre Brook

River Beam

River Thames

135

Annotated Bibliography and Further Reading

BOOKS AND OTHER PRINTED SOURCES

ESSAYS

Diane Watt: *The Earliest Women's Writing, Anglo-Saxon Literary Cultures and Communities* (Taylor & Francis, *Women's Writing* 20 (4), pp.537-554)*; Women, Writing and Religion in England and Beyond, 650–1100* (Bloomsbury Academic, 2019); 'Lost Books: Abbess Hildelith and the Literary Culture of Barking Abbey' (*Philological Quarterly*, 91(1) pp.1-22)

Vera Morton and Jocelyn Wogan-Browne: *Guidance for Women in Twelfth-Century Convents* (D.S. Brewer, 2003). Particularly, Morton's translations of Goscelin of St Bertin and Osbert of Clare, and Wogan-Browne's accompanying interpretive essay.

Jocelyn Wogan-Browne's introduction to *Language and Culture in Medieval Britain – The French of England c.1100–c.1500* (Cambridge University Press 2013): *What's in a Name: the 'French' of 'England'*

Lisa MC Weston: 'Sanctimoniales cum sanctimoniale: Particular Friendships and Female Community in Anglo-Saxon England' in: *Sex and Sexuality in Anglo-Saxon England*, Tempe, AZ. 2004 pp.35-62); 'The Saintly Female Body and Landscape of Foundation in Anglo-Saxon Barking' (*Medieval Feminist Forum: A Journal of Gender & Sexuality* 43, No. 2 (2007) pp.12-25); 'Women's Medicine, Women's magic: The Old English Metrical Childbirth Charms' (*Modern Philology* Vol. 92, No. 3 (Feb 1995) pp.279-293)

Jill Hamilton Clements: 'Writing and Commemoration in Anglo Saxon England' in: *Death in Medieval Europe*, ed. Joëlle Rollo-Koster, Routledge, 2017)

Laura Ashe: *Fiction and History in England, 1066–1200* (Cambridge University Press, 2011); *Early Fiction in England, from Geoffrey of Monmouth to Chaucer*, edited Laura Ashe (Penguin Classics, 2015)

Jennifer N. Brown and Donna Alfano Bussell (editors): *Barking Abbey and Medieval Literary Culture, Authorship and Authority in a Female Community* (Boydell & Brewer, York Medieval Press, 2012)

Duncan Robertson, 'Writing in the Textual Community: Clemence of Barking's Life of St. Catherine' (*French Forum*, Vol. 21, No.1 (1996) pp.5-28)

Eileen Power, *Medieval English Nunneries c 1275–1535* (Cambridge University Press, 1922)

Teresa L. Barnes, *A nun's life: Barking Abbey in the late-medieval and early modern periods* (Dissertations & Theses, Paper 948, 2004)

Jane Bliss, trans. *La Vie d'Edouard le Confesseur, by a Nun of Barking Abbey* (Exeter Medieval Texts & Studies, Liverpool University Press, 2014)

Hana Videen, *Blod, Swat, and Dreor: Material, Poetic, and Religious Discourses on Blood in Anglo-Saxon Literature* (unpublished PhD thesis, at academia.edu, 2016)

Andrea Maraschi, 'Red lights in the sky, hunger in sight. Aurora borealis and famine between experience and rhetoric in the early Middle Ages' (2018, *Revista de História da Sociedade e da Cultura* 18)

Katie Ann-Marie Bugyis, *The Ministries of Benedictine Women in England during the Central Middle Ages* (New York 2019, online edn, Oxford Academic)

Louise Tingle, *Royal Women, Intercession, and Patronage in England, 1328–1394* (thesis, Cardiff University, 2019)

Charles Creighton, *A History of Epidemics in Britain* (Cambridge: at the University Press, 1891)

James M. O'Toole, 'Commendatory Letters: An Archival Reading of the Venerable Bede', *The American Archivist* 61:2 (1998)

James A. Galloway, 'Fishing in Medieval England' (pp.629-642, *The Sea in History: the Medieval World* ed. Michel Balard, Océanides Association, Boydell Press 2017)

James A. Galloway and Jonathan S. Potts, 'Marine flooding in the Thames Estuary and tidal river c.1250–1450: impact and response' (pp. 370-379, *Area*, Vol. 39, No. 3, 2007)

Carla Rossi, 'The Withheld Name of Marie in the Epilogue of Guernes' Vie Saint Thomas' (*Il nome dell'Autore, Studi per Giuseppe Tavani*, I libri di Viella, 207, 2015 pp. 125-140); and 'Marie de France et les érudits de Cantorbéry': 1 (*Recherches Littéraires Médiévales*, Classiques Garnier, 2009) for her work on the identity of Marie de France, and horseback riding as metaphor for literary activity

June Hall McCash, 'La vie seinte Audree: A Fourth Text by Marie de France?' (*Speculum*, Vol. 77, No. 3 (2002) pp.744-777); and, with Judith Clark Barban, *The Life of Saint Audrey* (Mcfarland, 2006)

Anne Bagnall Yardley & Jesse D. Mann, 'The Liturgical Dramas for Holy Week at Barking Abbey' (*Medieval Feminist Forum*, Subsidia Series Vol. 3 2014)

Douglas Sugano (ed), *The N-Town Plays,* (Medieval Institute Publications, 2007)

Barbara Newman, 'Annihilation and Authorship: Three Women Mystics of the 1290s' (*Speculum*, Vol. 91, No.3, 2016)

Caroline Walker Bynum, 'Fast, Feast, and Flesh: The Religious Significance of Food to Medieval Women' (*Representations* No. 11, 1985)

Miranda Lynn Clemens (Sister Maria Parousia) *That they might sing the song of the lamb: The spiritual value of singing the liturgy for Hildegard of Bingen* (thesis, 2014)

Thomas Oswald Cockayne, *Leechdoms, Wortcunning, and Starcraft of Early England* (1866)

Dr Jessica Nelson, *Henry III and the rebuilding of Westminster Abbey* (National Archive, 2018)

Nancy Caciola, 'Mystics, Demoniacs, and the Physiology of Spirit Possession in Medieval Europe' (pp.268-306, *Comparative Studies in Society and History*, Vol. 42, No. 2, 2000)

Roger Rosewell, *Stained Glass in Anglo-Saxon England* (Woruldhord, University of Oxford)

Douglas Boyd, *Eleanor: April Queen of Aquitaine* (History Press Limited, 2005)

W Mark Omrod, 'The Trials of Alice Perrers' (pp.366-396, *Speculum*, Vol. 83, No. 2, 2008)

Karen K. Jambeck, 'The library of Alice Chaucer, Duchess of Suffolk: A Fifteenth-Century Owner of a "Boke of le Citee de Dames"' (*The Profane Arts of the Middle Ages: Commanding Women*, Vol. 7, No 2, 1998, pp.106-135)

Rev. Mackenzie E.C. Walcott, 'Inventory of St Mary's Benedictine Nunnery at Langley, Co. Leicester, 1485' (*Transactions of the Leicestershire Architectural and Archæological Society*, Volume IV, pp.117-122)

Patricia Demers, 'Margaret Roper & Erasmus' (*WWR Magazine*, Vol. 1, Issue 1, 2005)

OTHER TEXTS OF INTEREST

Bede, *Historia ecclesiastica gentis Anglorum,* translated by A.M. Sellar (George Bell and Sons, 1907)

Aldhelm, *De virginitate* translated by Michael Lapidge and Michael Herren in *Aldhelm – the Prose Works* (D.S. Brewer, 1979, 2009)

Anon., *The Anglo-Saxon Chronicle*

Hildegard of Bingen, *Physica, Causa et Curae, Scivias, Letters,* Mark Atherton translation in *Hildegard of Bingen – Selected Writings* (Penguin, 2001) Opening quotation is from *Scivias*, trans. by Columba Hart and Jane Bishop

The letters of Goscelin of St Bertin and Osbert of Clare, translated by Vera Morton in *Guidance for Women in Twelfth-Century Convents* (D.S. Brewer, 2003)

Goscelin of St Bertin's *Liber Confortatorius* translated by Monika Otter in *The Book of Encouragement and Consolation* (D.S. Brewer, 2004)

Various, *The Trotula,* 12th-century texts concerning female medicine, named for Trota of Salerno whose *De curis mulierum* is included therein, edited and translated by Monica H Green (University of Pennsylvania Press, 2001)

Jacopone da Todi, The Lauds, Serge and Elizabeth Hughes translation (Paulist Press International, US, 1981)

The OE poems: *Judith* and *Exodus,* translated by Dr Aaron K. Hostetter

Christine de Pizan, *The Book of the City of Ladies,* translated by Rosalind Brown-Grant (Penguin Classics, 1999); also, *The Treasure of the City of Ladies,* translated by Sarah Lawson (Penguin Classics, 2003)

Clémence of Barking, *La vie de sainte Catherine*

Marie de France – Poetry, translated by Dorothy Gilbert (W.W. Norton & Co. 2016)

The *Chronicon ex chronicis*, Florence of Worcester and/or John of Worcester

Daniel Defoe, *Poetical Essay on the Storm* (1703)

Anon., *Old English Lapidary*, on the precious stones of the Book of Revelation

The King James and Vulgate versions of the Bible

ONLINE MATERIALS

Gutenberg.org; JSTOR.org; and Academia.edu, were vital resources

Clerk of Oxford's blog about medieval England, all of which is fantastic but particularly her posts about Candlemas: https://aclerkofoxford.blogspot.com/

Kathryn Warner's notes on the murder of Maud Montagu's mother, Alice of Norfolk: http://edwardthesecond.blogspot.com/2019/04/the-life-and-tragic-death-of-alice-of.html

Diane Watt's blog about women's literary culture before the Conquest at Surrey University: https://blogs.surrey.ac.uk/early-medieval-women/

The Institute of Historical Research's website has been hugely helpful: https://www.british-history.ac.uk/ as has the website of Valence House Museum: https://valencehousecollections.co.uk/

Medieval poems in Anglo-Saxon, at the Internet Sacred Text Archive: https://www.sacred-texts.com/neu/ascp/index.htm

The *Prosopography of Anglo-Saxon England* (PASE) database of all recorded inhabitants of late-6th to late-11th century England, was useful for names: https://pase.ac.uk/

The Riddle Ages: Early Medieval Riddles, Translations and Commentaries, ed. Megan Cavell, with Matthias Ammon, Neville Mogford, Jennifer Neville, Alexandra Reider and Victoria Symons: https://theriddleages.com/

The Medieval Convent Drama project looks at performative activities undertaken by women within medieval convents, http://medievalconventdrama.org/

The following were useful for clothes/fabrics/etc: The V&A; the art historian and medievalist, Allan Barton; Rosalie Gilbert's Medieval Woman; and the historical needlework website: http://medieval.webcon.net.au/index.html

Della Farrant's blog post about Eleanor Cobham and Margery Jourdemayne: https://hidden-highgate.org/witch-queen-eleanor-cobham-bishops-lodge-highgate/

The diagram of Barking Abbey was made by Alfred W Clapham, following his excavation of the site in 1911. It was first published in *Essex Archaeological Transactions 12* (1913) in his article 'The Benedictine Abbey of Barking'. I have used the simplified version found in Vera Morton and Jocelyn Wogan-Browne's *Guidance for Women in Twelfth Century Convents* (Boydell & Brewer, 2012.) It is reproduced with the permission of both the Essex Society for Archaeology & History, and Boydell & Brewer.

The illustration of the Manor of Barking is reproduced with permission from *Victoria County History of the County of Essex: Volume 5* (London 1966) © University of London.

The Author

Ruth Wiggins is a British poet. She is based in East London but is happiest in the great outdoors, something which continues to inform her work. She studied English & Latin at Durham University and has three adult sons. Her poetry and essays have been included in UK and international journals and anthologies. *The Lost Book of Barkynge* is Ruth's first full collection. Ruth also has three pamphlets: *Myrtle* (Emma Press, 2014); *a handful of string* (Paekakariki Press, 2020); and *Menalhyl* (a private pressing of poems first published in *Long Poem Magazine* in 2016.)

Acknowledgements

I am firstly and foremostly indebted to Harriet Tarlo, without whose support and oversight this book would not have been possible, and for her reminder to revisit HD's *Helen in Egypt* at a crucial stage in the book's development. I am also grateful to Josephine Balmer for her encouragement, and to Laura Ashe for casting an early eye over my butchery of Anglo-Saxon, not to mention the many writers and historians whose scholarship opened the world of medieval Barking to me. I am grateful for the support of Tideway, but particularly my midwives-in-chief: Susie Campbell, Harriet Proudfoot, and Rachel Smith. Thank you to my family and friends for their bottomless patience and encouragement; and to Deryn Rees-Jones, Anja Konig and Nigel Pollitt. Lastly, I am beyond grateful to Tony Frazer for offering a home to my nuns and for dealing so kindly with them; and to Russell, who never lost faith.

Grateful thanks to the editors of *Blackbox Manifold* and *Lighthouse* for publishing earlier versions of 'The girl abbess'; 'Cusp & corbel'; 'Settle down muddy beds'; and 'Remedies'.

Printed in the USA
CPSIA information can be obtained
at www.ICGtesting.com
LVHW041059160823
755419LV00016B/95